RELUCTANT MISSIONARY

RELUCTANT MISSIONARY

by

EDITH BUXTON

HODDER AND STOUGHTON
LONDON SYDNEY AUCKLAND TORONTO

DEDICATED

to the memory of
the thirty-one missionaries who
in this same area lost their
lives as a result of the Congo
Rebellion of 1964

 ISBN *0 340 17690 3.* *Printed in Great Britain for Hodder and Stoughton Limited, St. Paul's House, Warwick Lane, London EC4P 4AH by Richard Clay (The Chaucer Press), Ltd, Bungay, Suffolk*

CONTENTS

FOREWORD

I HAVE known for years that my sister-in-law, Edith Buxton, has a natural gift for writing, as for speaking. Thirty years ago I tried to get her to write her Father, C. T. Studd's life. Her own little booklet of self-revelation, *The Three Flies,* has sold by the tens of thousands, and as soon as she began to describe some incident from the platform, the audience was living it over again with her.

Reading the first draft of this book, which has taken her ten years to complete, my son Daniel,[1] with his considerable knowledge of English literature, wrote, 'The gamut of emotions were mine as I read it. I cannot too highly praise it. Your ability to depict and portray enlivens whatever you talk about and stirs the imagination. Not many people can express themselves interestingly. You do more than that and flash light on hidden paths in the forests of all men's needs.'

This is true. Whether it is a flash-back into a young girl's glimpses of her life in a West End Victorian household, shot through it all she writes with almost a Dickensian humour; or fascinating descriptions, with the brilliant colouring of a Manet painting, of a white woman among her Congolese friends in the years of primitive living in the Congo forests which have gone for ever: these in themselves are almost a piece of social history.

But there is far more than this. Edith wrote with serious purpose. This is a life story—of God in a life—in

1. Daniel Grubb, Ph.D. (Univ. of Michigan).

several lives.

The piercing element in her descriptions of herself is her radical honesty. She does not paint a beautiful picture of herself. You would hardly realize, unless you look at her photograph, the radiant beauty that she was in form and feature, which made men turn to look at her on the streets and artists want to paint her. Stage by stage she expresses what God made her to see of her own self, gathered into one phrase by the title of the book. She shows us much of the ugliness of the human self, common to all of us, in its self-activities; but the seeing eye will catch another picture—of a dedicated self, more dedicated than she admits even to herself, and captured by Christ, when she could have chosen a marriage of wealth, a husband any girl would dream of, the broad acres of a county family and estate. She lived for Christ with a husband who had her whole heart, but whose single-hearted devotion to God and world need made her feel like a spiritual pygmy beside him; then shock and suffering and disillusionment only gradually brought her, by the end chapters of the book, into the full sunlight of the realization of the God of love who had really always been in her inmost centre.

The biographies of great men often need sidelights shone on them by those who knew them to put them in full perspective, and Edith does this in amusing and certainly in penetrating fashion for her famous father. Readers of C. T. Studd will get a number of new insights into the human 'C.T.', and this will be one of the main values of this book, especially to the many for whom he is the father-founder of the now widespread Worldwide Evangelization Crusade. Both he and Alfred Buxton, who was co-pioneer with C. T. Studd, stand out in living colours, not losing but gaining stature by a daughter's and wife's candid comments. It may be that this is the last intimate glimpse into an era of missionary pioneering in the heart of Africa, from which the new Africa and new African Church of Christ is now gloriously emerging.

NORMAN P. GRUBB

1

FROM CHINA

THERE was no doubt that we four girls had been landed with unique parents.

My Father, Charles T. Studd, in the days of W. G. Grace, captained the Eton and Cambridge cricket elevens, then played for All-England in Australia. As a result of the Moody and Sankey Evangelical Revival of 1880 he underwent a religious experience which changed his life. He gave up everything and went as a missionary to China in 1885. Here he met my Mother.

Priscilla Stewart came of a large family in Belfast, where her father and uncles owned linen mills. She had a similar change of heart as had my Father and felt called to China as a missionary. They met in Shanghai and were married there in 1886. The story goes that they trailed off into the interior of China with a few pots and pans and a roll of bedding.

We were all born in the heart of China, fed three times a day on birds' seed, with none of us developing a singing voice between us. Ten years my parents spent in China. Then Father got typhoid and was ordered home. His friends doubted whether he would ever reach England.

'There goes a dying man,' they said.

He recovered, however, but it left him with asthma which was to trouble him at times for the rest of his life.

Mother's hands were full on the journey with a seriously ill husband and four children. And there was added danger. It was the time of the war between China and

Japan. The Chinese thought they were the centre of the world and every other country outside was referred to as 'The Kingdom of the Foreign Devils'. It had also been spread around that Father was one of those who had rebelled against China. Travelling by junk down the Yellow River near Tientsin, an ugly crowd had gathered to see the 'foreign devils'.

While we were hidden below, my eldest sister, Grace, aged six, escaped from my Mother and made her way on deck. Leaning casually over the side of the boat, she surveyed the crowd with interest. Neither her tiny pigtail nor her small Chinese jacket could disguise the fact that she was a 'foreign devil'.

'What is your age, and your name? And, have you any food?' they shouted—which is the usual Chinese greeting. To their astonishment, she answered all their questions in Chinese. From anger, they now paused to admire. They then arranged for relays of Chinese to advance and ask the same questions. At the end they summed it up thus: 'You see, this child talks our language because she eats our food.' And no harm came to any of us that day.

My first recollection is of standing in the middle of the cabin floor at Tilbury, in the London Docks, and Father buttoning my stays on back to front. Although only three, I told him in no uncertain Chinese how wrong he was. I can see my Mother's laughing face leaning over the upper bunk. On arrival I have vague visions of Pauline in Mother's arms, and growlers, and luggage. Having despatched all of us ahead, my Father and his brother Kynaston jumped into the last remaining cab. He must have eyed this array of mission children with some misgivings as to the future, and he now turned to my Father and said, 'Charlie, how are you off for money?' To which my father replied, 'I think I have ten shillings in my pocket!'

2

TEDWORTH

I NEVER knew my grandfather, Edward Studd. He must have been a man of some spirit for I felt his presence everywhere, even as a child, though he must have been dead for sixteen years when we arrived from China. Two portraits of him hung at Hyde Park Gardens. One showed him aged twenty-seven at the time of his first marriage in India, when in 1846 he had bought two indigo plantations, Seriah and Dholi, a few miles from Muzufferpore in the Province of Behar. The other painting showed him at the age of thirty-seven, when he met my grandmother in Calcutta on one of his many visits to Thomas and Co., a firm which sold his indigo.

Standing the other day before this second portrait, signed W. G. Turner and now in the keeping of his eldest grandson,[1] I noted the black velvet cravat, the diamond pin, the wavy hair, the curly good-humoured mouth and the most engaging twinkle in his eyes. He was a very good-looking young man with a masculine stamp about him. He must have had a good business head too, for it was not long before he amassed two fortunes in indigo at a time when it was the only blue dye in the world.

His first wife, Margaret Hudson, died at Seriah in 1853 in her early thirties, leaving him with four small children. But he loved them and life became happy once again in the comfortable plantation home at Dholi. His

1. Sir Eric Studd, Bart.

humour reasserted itself, and he became known for his daring pranks.

On one occasion he emptied a bottle of red ink into the shower in a visitor's bathroom. The perforated drum that held the water hung over the bath and his friend coming in hot from riding pulled the chain with pleasurable anticipation. No amount of scrubbing was of any use and he turned up bright pink for dinner that night.

On another occasion after a dinner with friends, their buggys drawn up in front of the house awaiting their departure, he slipped down the long wide steps to the drive and tied the reins of one of the horses to the collar. The visitor emerged and took his seat in his carriage. The animal charged down the drive, and the man's cries of alarm as he pulled on the reins, only caused Grandfather to double up with mirth as he stood with his friends on the steps to see the fun.

He risked his own life too, without a thought. He was the only man in memory who was known to ride down a wolf and kill it single-handed with a spear.

Meanwhile, my future grandmother, Dora Thomas, was tossing up with her three sisters to decide who should go on a visit to Calcutta to her two brothers. Neither Hannah nor Frizzie wanted to go because they were already being courted and Mary was always delicate, so undoubtedly Dora was the one to go. Their home was Blestoe Castle[1] in Bedfordshire, where they lived with their father, John Thomas.

The day came a few weeks later when Dora, packed and ready, kissed her father and three sisters goodbye, and sallied forth on the long journey to India. Arriving in Calcutta, she was met by the brothers, and as the family firm, Thomas and Company, sold most of the indigo from

1. An old Elizabethan house owned by the late St. John family and rented to John Thomas.

Behar, it was not long before she found herself in the company of the handsome pleasure-loving Edward Studd, who had come in from Dholi to arrange one of his usual sale transactions. Dora did not have the same good looks as her new friend, Edward Studd, but she was a striking figure of a young woman, with dignity and poise beyond her years, the most glorious eyes the colour of a tiger skin, with charcoal lines round the amber of the iris. She had well-arched eyebrows and beautiful dark brown shining hair. It may have been those lovely eyes that decided Edward to leave his plantations and return home for good. There must have been great jubilation, the lights of Bletsoe burning late into the night, when Dora brought home her gay and handsome young man. They were married at Bletsoe village church in 1856.

The young couple lost no time and settled in the Shires (for Edward Studd had a passion for horses), first at Stratton Hill House in 1860 and then at Hallerton Hall, Netheravon, Wiltshire. Here he was in the saddle morning, noon and night, and soon took over the duties of M.F.H.[1] During these years four sons were born to them, my Father being the third. At five and six years old they were strapped into the saddle and joined the family to follow hounds.

Edward with his zest and initiative in forging ahead must have been some husband to keep up with. However, Dora was as good a horseman as he. No sooner had they all mastered some of the stiffest fences in Leicestershire than he turned his attention to racing and to the training and breeding of horses. Tattersalls[2] saw him in and out almost daily. This new venture needed a property large enough to provide him with practice gallops and a

1. Master of Foxhounds.
2. The famous London sale ring for buying and selling horses.

race-course. One can imagine Edward scanning the daily papers for the kind of place he wanted and how his eye may have been caught by an advertisement like this: 'Spacious Georgian Manor House to let in the county of Wiltshire, situated in extensive parkland. Mile-long driveway up to imposing entrance of four stone pillars rising to the first floor. Gracious reception rooms . . . apply to owner, Assheton Smith.' However the advertisement may have been worded, Tedworth itself must have more than fulfilled Edward's expectations. It was a house of charm, like a lady in white reclining gracefully on a green lawn on a summer's day.

It was at Tedworth, which he took over in 1860, that Edward made a superb race-course in the park and built up a stud of twenty horses which he bred for racing. Not content with winning several steeplechases, he set his heart on the Grand National, and won this race with a horse called Salamander in 1866. Edward had been on the look-out for horses in Ireland when he saw in a gipsy's drove a brood-mare in foal. He lost no time in making a bid for her, and eventually she was shipped off to England and in due course threw a stallion, and this was Salamander. It was Dora who spotted the quality of the colt and declared he was too good for hunting and should be trained as a chaser. Five of Edward's horses ran in the Grand National at different times. In his well-thumbed notebook we find this list:

'1865 Horse did not finish
1866 Grand National won on Salamander
1867 Shangarry ended third
1869 Despatch came in sixth
1871 Despatch came in second
1872 Despatch came in third

1873 Alice Lee, out of Rosalba,[1] finished fifth...'

On the night when Salamander won the Grand National, all the family gathered for a celebration dinner, at which Edward presented Dora with an enormous round diamond brooch, two inches in diameter. The two eldest girls were given brooches of Salamander's head beautifully carved in mother-of-pearl and painted, caught under a crystal glass and surrounded by diamonds.

When ultimately Salamander fell at a fence, broke his leg and had to be destroyed, the whole family turned up at dinner in black. There can be no argument; they were all dead serious about horse-racing.

It was at Tedworth that their last two sons were born. This brought Dora's family up to six sons and one daughter. The three eldest boys had a governess. One day they went to their father and said, 'We insist on going to school; she won't let us walk out with walking sticks.' So off they went to a preparatory school at Cheam, though my Father was only seven years old at the time.

One day, some fifty years after Father lived there, I visited Tedworth[2] and stepped up those two shallow steps under the porticoed and pillared entrance into the first hallway, flanked by gun rooms and cloakrooms. I passed on into the second hall, looking up at the fan-shaped staircase to the first floor. My eyes followed the balcony encircling the first landing. Behind me, as I stood there, was the drawing-room; the rose coloured satin was still on the walls, some of it tearing away in strips so that I

1. Rosalba was the mare Edward bought in Ireland. She threw 28 foals in 29 years.

2. Now known as Tidworth Officers Club, Headquarters Southern Command.

longed to pocket a piece. The large white fireplace, the tall broad windows reaching from top to bottom looking out on the lawns and garden, gave the room beautiful proportions.

I wondered, as I stood there, about Edward Studd. Had he lingered over the beauties of this home when he changed his way of life? Had he heard the echo of familiar sounds, the smack of a cricket bat on the ball and the shout of boys at play? Had he, too, stood in these windows and reflected on the leisure of life, the luxury when no money problems existed and the next thing to do was only what you wanted to do?

And my Father, when he lay tossing with typhoid fever in China, did he have visions of Tedworth in the early morning, of being at the stables getting ready to ride, of the feel of a good horse as he cantered away into the clear crisp morning, and of the beauty of the rolling countryside as he chased the fox? Did he think of the happy companionship of those five brothers; days at Eton, the sound of steps going up to Chapel and the rise and swell of voices at Evensong; the marquees and coaches up at Lords; the first mouthful of strawberries and cream on a June day, and coming home to Tedworth of an evening? Did he remember the bustle of servants bringing in some wonderful meal, the playroom noisy with the older boys, the nurseries of the younger ones, the maids bright with starch and soap, old scenes that must have been etched on his mind with the poignancy of time beyond recall?

They both, father and son, did everything they put their hand to with a will, never lacking in courage and determination, whether riding a horse at a fence, or meeting any other challenge. But perhaps, as with dedicated men, there was no room in their thoughts for nostalgia or regret.

The sergeant-major in charge of the Officers' mess led

me to his office and spread a plan of the house before me.

'See here,' he said, pointing to a row of rooms to the right of the garden door, 'here were the library, boudoir, writing room, flower room and so on.'

In mind I recaptured the scene. Dora, her head bowed over some letter she was writing, the long winter morning stretching away ahead, the fire burning busily in the grate. There would be the visits of housekeeper, nanny, and nursemaids about arrangements for the day, perhaps her two youngest sons playing on the hearth. Suddenly I felt a sense of finality; the day that for Dora seemed so secure would end. It was as if I looked over her shoulder that morning at the spindly handwriting and knew—what she could not know—the manner in which the substantial things around her, and she herself, would change and cease to be. As I wandered from room to room all this worked inside me like a brew, and I felt in my heart a closeness and a love for Dora and Edward Studd and my Father that I had never had before.

For the Studd family, the quiet years slipped by; there was hunting in the winter, and in the summer it was cricket—cricket practice, cricket matches, cricket weeks. Edward had a first-class cricket pitch made on a knoll at the back of the house, and Dora found her garden sadly neglected because the gardeners were always being called off work during the summer holidays to bowl and field for the boys. For refreshment they raided the dairy and drank their own concoction of ginger beer and cream. Continually fortified with this rich brew, the three eldest grew to superb manhood and achieved fame at Eton by all being in the cricket eleven together.

With his growing stables, Edward's visits to Tattersalls became more frequent, and he decided he needed a town house. In 1875 he bought 2 Hyde Park Gardens, a fine

Victorian mansion on the north side of the park.

Life might have continued indefinitely along these peaceful and comfortable lines—Edward happily dividing his time between his family and his horses—if it had not been for an incident involving a friend of Edward's which took place in Ireland in 1876.

> Away in Dublin in the year 1876 the Punchestown races were over. Crowds were returning homeward from the famous Irish Derby. Among them was a friend of Edward's, a man named Vincent who had owned a neighbouring plantation in India. He had the misfortune to miss his boat back to England from Kingstown Harbour by five minutes. Faced with a free evening before him he stepped out from his hotel and saw over a theatre the names of Moody and Sankey. Wondering what strange company this was, he went in. It was not long before he realized it was a religious show and the two men on the platform were Americans.[1]

He would have retreated in haste, but the beauty of the singer's voice and the strangeness of the then little-known hymn he was singing, riveted him to the spot:

But none of the ransomed ever knew
How deep were the waters crossed,
Nor how dark was the night that the Shepherd passed through
Ere he found the sheep that was lost.

What was it to be a lost sheep, he thought, and what did it mean to be ransomed? He soon found out. For Moody who had come over to evangelize the British Isles

1. *C. T. Studd, Cricketer and Pioneer,* Norman Grubb, Lutterworth Press, London.

was no pi, long-winded preacher. His sermons were very much to the point and never lasted more than twenty minutes.

He went back to his hotel, moved as he had never been before and to thoughts he scarcely knew existed within him. Instead of catching the boat next day he stayed on, going to hear Moody each evening. Then there came a time when he found himself joining a crowd of people going to the 'enquiry room'. It is on record that, like his short sermons, this terse conversation passed between Moody and Vincent:

'Mr. Vincent, do you believe that Christ died for you?'

'I do,' he replied.

'Then,' said Moody, 'thank Him.'

He did, on his knees, and left the room a different person.

Vincent returned to London, and finally Moody and Sankey arrived there too and set up in the Drury Lane Theatre.

Edward had meanwhile written to Vincent about a horse that he was entering for one of the big races. 'If you are a wise man,' he wrote, 'you will come to the race and put every penny you can on my horse.'

Eventually they met in London and, while driving to Tattersalls together Edward said, 'How much money did you put on my horse?'

'Nothing,' said Vincent.

'Well, you are the biggest fool I ever saw. Didn't I tell you what a good horse he was?' said Edward. In spite of this sharp exchange of words Edward said, 'Though you are a fool, come and dine with me. The family are all in the country.'

So, dinner over at 2 Hyde Park Gardens, the two friends sat in the light of candles softly illuminating the white tablecloth, cracking nuts and passing the port.

Edward suddenly said, 'Where shall we go to amuse ourselves, or I'll go anywhere you suggest?'

'How about Drury Lane?' said Vincent.

'What,' said Edward, 'isn't that where those fellows Moody and Sankey are? The papers have been full of them and I mean to hear them, but for a start this is not Sunday. Let's go to a theatre or concert.'

'Now,' said Vincent, with a twinkle, 'you are a man of your word and you said you would go where I chose, and I choose Drury Lane.'

Edward gave in.

The theatre was already crowded out but Vincent was determined that having got Edward so far he would get him in; he beckoned to a steward, and scribbled on a card and got a message to Moody.

This was the message: 'I have a wealthy sporting friend with me; I will never get him here again if you don't get us seats tonight.'

The steward returned and took them through the green door, across the stage, and settled them in the front row of the stalls. Edward never took his eyes off Moody till he had finished his address, and he said afterwards, 'I will come and hear this man again.' In that short time his eyes had been opened, and he recognized within himself a longing which his present mode of life would never satisfy.

Edward Studd was now fifty-six, his hair greying, but his eyes still looked out direct and clear under the strongly marked eyebrows. Looking at a photograph of him, I see his nose is well-chiselled and he wears mutton chop whiskers. His spotted tie is broadly knotted under a butterfly collar. A white waistcoat is folded inside a double-breasted jacket, bordered at the lapels with braid and well tailored over his broad shoulders. He is still as fine a figure of a man as you would wish to see. Yet a decisive moment in

Edward's life had arrived. Not only did he experience a religious conversion, but his whole way of life, his established values changed in order to express his new faith, with all the energy and enthusiasm of which he was capable.

While this was going on in London, the three eldest boys were winning their spurs at Eton. So far as is known this is the only time that three brothers were ever in the Eton Eleven together. One day a letter arrived from Edward saying he had arranged for them all to come up and meet him in London. The boys thought nothing of it, just a visit to the theatre as a prize for doing so well at cricket, no doubt. But on arrival they were swept off to hear Moody. Shaken as they were to have to go to a pi-show, and not on a Sunday, it was nothing to the shock of the change they saw in their Father.

'In the afternoon of that day,' wrote one of his sons later, 'Father had been more full of a thing that takes possession of a man's heart and head more than anything else—the passion for racing; and in the evening he was a changed man.'

He withdrew from the turf, giving a horse to each of his elder sons as a hunter, and then sold the remainder. He cleared out the hall at Tedworth and put in chairs and benches; then he rode round the countryside to urge his neighbours to come in on Sunday evenings. They came in their hundreds, filling up the staircase to the first floor, leaning over the balconies to hear the fellows he got to come from London to speak to them. Moody himself came. Dora was fussed at his coming and dreaded the fateful question, 'Mrs. Studd, are you saved?' So she surrounded herself with all her family, and when Mr. Moody came in he said, with pleasurable surprise, 'Mrs. Studd, what a wonderful family you have!' This quite won her heart and she had no more fear.

As Edward had never done anything by halves, he now threw himself into saving the souls of his friends and relations. The evangelical message of those revival days was forthright, and as delivered by Edward it was more like a sword-thrust than a message.

'Are you saved? If not, you will go to Hell and that's flat.'

He strode round one day to Gloucester Square where his brother-in-law, George, lived. No sooner had he got it off his chest than he was promptly shown the front door and George slammed it on him with a bang. He never entered No. 32 again.

His son Herbert remembers a morning at Tedworth when he accompanied his Father to the stables, and Edward shouted across the lawn to a gardener, 'Giles, are you saved?' Though Herbert told me this when he was seventy, indignation at the embarrassment he felt was still in his voice.

Edward continued to attend Moody's meetings; he would come out at half time and send in the coachman and footman, and hold the horses himself. He spoke fearlessly to anyone and everyone on salvation through trusting in Christ. When he could not speak, he wrote to his friends. One man, an agnostic who kept a shop in Piccadilly, was so faithfully dealt with that his son said afterwards, 'I never saw my father so angry in my life.' Nor was it words only. He gave generously wherever there was need, even to the gift of a house in America to his friend Moody, and he contributed largely to the founding of the Moody Bible Institute in Chicago for the training of missionaries for the foreign field.[1]

Edward died in 1878 at the early age of fifty-eight. He was on his way to one of Moody's meetings and stopped

1. Since its inception many thousands of missionaries have been trained and sent out over the world.

the carriage suddenly when he remembered he had meant to bring one of the grooms. He alighted and told the rest to drive on. It was late and he ran all the way back. This caused him to burst a blood vessel, and I was told as a child that it was while being carried up the stairs to his bedroom that he died.

Edward only lived for two years after his conversion, but it was said of him that in those two years he had worked wholeheartedly for the Kingdom of God on earth and accomplished more than most Christians do in a lifetime.

My father, known then by his initials 'C.T.', was the third son. He had captained the Eton Eleven in 1879 and the Cambridge University Eleven in 1882. He was accorded in the latter year (*vide* the *Cricketing Annual*) 'the premier position as an all-round cricketer for the second year in succession'. In 1884 he played for the Gentlemen of England with W. G. Grace and others, and it is interesting to recall that he was a member of the famous All-England team which played at the Oval against the Australians when they beat England for the first time. It was on this occasion that the facetious epitaph was written: 'In affectionate remembrance of English cricket which died at the Oval ... N.B. The body will be cremated and the ashes taken to Australia.'

Later he was in the team which went back to Australia to retrieve the Ashes. During this tour England won two of the three matches and came back in triumph with the Urn.

C.T. was not only a born cricketer, he made a serious business of it. In applying himself to the game he went all out to get to the top of the tree. In so doing he learnt lessons of courage, self-denial and endurance which were to stand him in good stead in the hard life he was to choose later. To this day his portrait hangs in that hard-won place, 'The Gallery of Famous Etonians'. You will find it at the end of the corridor near the Scholars' Hall, and listed in the archives as 'Cricketer and Pioneer'.

C.T. was converted at Tedworth soon after his father had his miraculous change of heart. A young man had come down for the weekend to speak at the Sunday evening gathering in the hall. He had no athletic ability and could not even ride a horse; the boys thought him a bit of a milksop. But it was the milksop who was the means of persuading Father to 'decide for Christ', though the main influence that had been working towards this end was his own father.

I once at an evening meeting at Wimbledon heard C.T. tell the story of his conversion. The room was packed to suffocation, mostly with young people. He had that sense of mirth which was infectious and usually began his talks with some amusing story. He once said to me, 'I'll be bound more people are pulled into the Kingdom of Heaven on the rope of mirth than by any other means.' He told them that night, 'I had the good fortune to meet a real live play-the-game Christian. It was my own father. But it did make one's hair stand on end. Everyone in the house had a dog's life of it until they got converted. I was not altogether pleased with him. He used to come to my room at night and ask if I was saved. After a time I used to sham sleep when I saw the door open, and in the day I crept round the other side of the house when I saw him coming. When we boys came home from Eton we did not understand what had come over him, but Father kept continually telling us that he was "born again". We thought that he was just born upside down because he was always asking about our souls and we did not like it.'

After his father's death, C.T. went up to Cambridge

and did little about living out his Christianity. He had received Christ as his Saviour at Tedworth but as yet had made no dedication of his life to God for service to his fellowmen. Cricket filled his life. It was in 1882 that he reached the height of his form. Though only a third year man at the University, he rose to the very top of the cricket world, amateur and professional alike. It is doubtful whether any other undergraduate in the history of cricket has ever done such a thing.

Lillywhites Annual said that year: 'C.T. Studd must be given the premier position among the batsmen of 1882, and it would be difficult to instance three finer innings played by so young a cricketer against the best bowling of the day, than his three-figure scores against Australia and the Players.'

In bowling, only one in all England, the professional Peate, had taken more wickets and was ranked before him. Many people considered that the Cambridge Eleven of 1882 was one of the finest that has ever represented a University. In the most famous match of the season, Cambridge was the first side to beat the Australians. The Australians were only beaten twice that season. The same year, 1882, with the three Studd brothers playing, Cambridge also beat Lancashire—champion county—and Oxford.

Incidentally, it was *Punch* who gave them the nickname 'The Set of Studds' and there was a banker who went one better than *Punch*. He had three gold studs on his evening shirt engraved with the initials of the three brothers. Whoever made top score of the day was top in the shirt that night.

C.T. finished his brilliant career at Cambridge as captain. During his four years in the Eleven, in first-class matches alone he scored 1,852 runs (Lillywhites Record).

After Cambridge, he studied for the Bar and lived in

London with his mother. Then his second brother, George, to whom he was especially attached, was taken ill with pneumonia and was believed to be dying. In a small room overlooking the gardens on the third floor at Hyde Park Gardens he lay on the brass bedstead tossing with fever. It was in this room that I slept as a girl and I often thought of Uncle George. The room had seen little change. I remember a picture that hung above the washstand. As I brushed my teeth every night it made a great impression on me. It was of the abandoned cross of Christ, and three Eastern travellers are looking at it in curiosity. The half-torn parchment is still nailed to it—Pilate's edict, 'The King of the Jews'.

It was here, the gaslight burning low, that my Father watched over George night after night. Father was still in his early twenties and had known most of the pleasures and honours this world can give. I have heard him tell of the thoughts that went through his mind in the night as he sat by his brother's bedside: 'Now, what is all this popularity of the world worth to George? What is all the fame and flattery worth? What is it worth to possess all the riches of the world when a man comes to face eternity? Worth, worth, worth,' the word kept repeating itself in his mind and with it that phrase: 'Vanity of vanities. What shall it profit a man if he gain the whole world and lose his own soul?'

George was to recover; but something had been reawakened in C.T. and he went to hear Moody once again. The religious revival in this country was now at its height. What transpired between him and Moody is not on record, but the outcome was that he gave up cricket and dedicated himself, as Edward had done, to 'saving souls', and ultimately he chose to go as a missionary to China.

During the year following this dedication, he was tireless in speaking up and down the country. He was no orator, but he had a forthright manner of speaking. A story goes that on one of these occasions (a Sunday afternoon at a Police Institute) he hummed and hawed so much, standing first on one foot and then on the other, that the Institute Committee gathered outside after and said, 'We cannot possibly have this young man again.' However, when a few Sundays later a speaker failed, and the Committee asked the policemen whom they would like to fill in the gap, they said with one voice, 'That chap Studd.'

'Whatever makes you want him?' they asked.

'Well, we understood him; he spoke straight out from the shoulder.'

His speaking must have improved for I can remember his never having a Sunday free. His engagements would take him all over Britain—men's meetings, chapels, nonconformist churches, even speaking from the lectern in Church of England services. Only once was he persuaded to put on a surplice and speak from the pulpit!

The stir that was caused when he went at the age of 26 as a missionary to China was considerable. Seven of them went together, for they had all been friends at Cambridge, and they became known as 'The Cambridge Seven'. They were a remarkable collection. Stanley Smith, the stroke of the Cambridge boat, and the stroke oar of one of the trial eights, a Dragoon Guardsman, an officer of the Royal Artillery, and the son and heir of a titled family in Norfolk. In the history of missions no band of volunteers has caught the imagination of the public as much as these seven. Queen Victoria was pleased to receive a booklet giving their testimonies. Such was the stir among the universities that their sailing had to be put off so that they could go to Edinburgh and speak at the urgent request of the leading professors. In a hall packed with 2,000 students they were cheered again and again as they rose to speak. One of the medical students wrote of the occasion: 'Stanley Smith was eloquent, but Studd could not speak a bit—It was the fact of his devotion to Christ which told and he, if anything, made the greatest impression.'

The deep stir, however, and strongest opposition was to come from his own family. It had been a shock when his father had been converted, but that one of them should become a missionary was the last straw.

At last his eldest brother, who had been the leader of the trio of brothers, came to him and said, 'Charlie, you are out every night at meetings; Mother never sees you; you are breaking her heart.'

Father's answer to this was, 'I do not want to be pig-headed and just go on my own, I only want God's will.'

That night he could not sleep for the echoing of the phrase, 'Ask of me, and I will give thee the heathen for thine inheritance, and the uttermost part of the earth for thy possession.'

'I knew it was God's voice speaking to me,' he said, 'and that I had received my marching orders for China.'

But seeing his mother's tears and in an agony of conflicting loyalties, one night he walked out to wander the streets. It was while standing beside a lamp post under the flickering gas light that in desperation he asked God to speak to him again. He took out his Testament, opened it at random and read just where it fell open these words, 'And a man's foes shall be they of his own household.'

From that moment he never looked back. And go to China he did in the year 1885 and that is where my sisters and I were born. My faded Birth Certificate is beside me as I write this: born September 23, 1892, in the inland Chinese town of Lu-ngan-Fu, Shansi, Signed by C. T. C. Werner, Pro-Consul at Tientsin.

3

LIFE IN HYDE PARK GARDENS

It was to my Grandmother's house in Hyde Park Gardens that we came and were put in a set of rooms on the third floor in charge of a nanny and a nursemaid. We understood no English, they no Chinese. Soon quarrels broke out between the English and the Chinese, my eldest sister settling the matter by marshalling us before her down the passage and locking us all in the bathroom. We were only persuaded, after much negotiation through the door by my Mother, to come out and face the wrathful nanny.

My Grandmother became the Fairy Godmother of us all, and Uncle Willie Bradshaw (married to Father's only sister) educated us first in Switzerland and then with his own children in Sherborne. It goes to their eternal credit that they did this with such grace and kindness, when neither of them agreed with what my Father had done in giving away his inheritance. Under this vow of poverty he toured Britain and America, and no hall or church was ever empty—'he preached Christ as though he never would preach again, and as a dying man to dying men'. Meanwhile my Mother, upstairs at Hyde Park Gardens, rustling softly in the silk dress given her by her mother-in-law, wept silent tears as she longed for the days in China. She was a woman of beauty and great spirit and the brothers-in-law delighted in chaffing her. She, with her quick wit and Irish sauce, soon won my Uncle Kynnie.

He admired her so much that he had her sketched on a china plaque. Her calm, lovely shaped face looks steadily at you, two gold buttons fastening her simple Chinese jacket at the neck.

Every evening, dressed in viyella, all agog and smocked to the eyes, we four descended in solemn array to the drawing-room to meet the family, who had come to tea. This was no laughing matter—Uncle Peter teased the life out of us. We had an answer for everything. We stood our ground and jabbered back in pidgin English and Chinese, to the roars of laughter of uncles and aunts.

I can see us now: my eldest sister Grace, with the frightened eyes of a little deer, ever ready to protect us; Dorothy, 'a very tea kettle for cosiness'; myself—the complete show-off; and Pauline, who looked like a little angel but screamed her head off at the sight of English food. This embarrassed us considerably.

Hyde Park Gardens is now a block of luxury flats, but one Sunday evening when I passed by the whole row of houses was empty except two. The ivy on the mews wall opposite fluttered in the wind, and leaves leapt up from the gutter to the pavement. It was all inexpressibly dreary, I stepped up the two once white steps to the double-fronted door and tried to push open the letter-box, but it had been nailed down. I went into the area; it was full of workmen's planks and sand.

Those days were finished now. Everything said so. Through the window, where once one saw the bright fire in the housekeeper's sanctum, there was only a rusty rotting grate. The cupboards that held the jam, row upon row, were empty, the doors hanging open . . .

Long ago a table stood in the middle of the small room where Mrs. Miles, the cook, and the butler, Ryall, had their meals away from the rest of the staff. Down the spiral back staircase from the upper hall there was a long stone passage, and having passed the housekeeper's room you came to the wine cellar. There Ryall would carefully choose what Granny wanted from the dusty iron shelves, and wipe off the cobwebs from the bottles. I was once invited into his pantry, where the table was scrubbed into grooves, and the lift worked up to the dining-room. It gave me an idea, and it was not long before we sisters found an opportunity to get inside the lift and work each other up to the dining-room. We must have done this without being caught, for I never remember any repercussions. Opposite the butler's pantry was the footman's. Here to be sure Charles, in a green baize apron, would be polishing silver. I felt shy of the footman; he was tall and good-looking. I got away as soon as I could. Down a few steps you came to the kitchen—an enormous table filled the middle of this large stone-flagged room. Our nightmare here was Polly, the parrot which my Father had brought back from Australia. His shriek was so loud it hurt your ears. My one fear was that they would let him out and then he would chase us round the kitchen table and peck our legs. Ryall was the only one who could make him sing. Presently, after some coaxing, would come the first notes of 'Home Sweet Home', very slow and very sweet. He swayed from side to side and slurred up and down the melody with a tremulous sobbing that moves me still to remember.

Mrs. Miles might be making a tart while this was going on, on a table so large that eight cooks could have stood in a row either side. Her tarts were always packed tight with fruit and domed in shape, and covered with sugar. In the dining-room above, Granny would cut them on Sundays. She would hold the knife poised and pierce the tart at the centre. There was no collapse of the pastry—it was still firm and sugary. Ryall, waiting in respectful silence, would remove the helping of tart and close on his tracks would come the little silver tray with sugar and cream. The dumpy jug was only half full of very thick cream. It was difficult not to take too much, and if you did, Ryall would jiggle the tray to make you stop.

From the dining-room, french windows gave on to the terrace which overlooked the long reach of gardens bordering Bayswater Road. On sunny days you could sit there, for on either side were iron seats, and the key to the door into the gardens was kept in some secret recess known only to Ryall.

The morning began with family prayers. If it was winter a bright fire would be burning in the grate, which reflected in the brass eagles on either side. They held the tongs and poker, and the steel and brass shone to distraction. My Father sat at the table, already spread for breakfast, with the Bible open. There would be the sound of the fire crackling, and the rustle of Mrs. Miles' starched dress and apron as she led the way in, followed by Ryall and Charles, then Jenkins and Roland, the housemaids. Roland was dark and saucy. We liked her better than Jenkins, who always answered the searching questions of little girls with, 'It wouldn't do to say, Miss.'

There followed the droning of Father's voice, and far away the intermittent sounds of Bayswater Road. A hansom would come by, clippity clop, then a growler or a bus.

When I was very little, Aunt Fanny would lift me on to her knee and here I would listen to the creak of her stays as she breathed and the straining of her tight black silk dress. I watched her pearl and diamond brooch rise and fall on her softly breathing bosom. Slanting rays of light came in through the high windows, the pictures on the walls lighting up in unbelievable reality: the horse and rider leaping over a fence; the dogs and gamekeeper, a picture so large it nearly covered one wall.

Calm and dignified, my Grandmother on the sofa by the fire, in her grey wig and black satin, would be breathing in and out like Aunt Fanny with the same soft intriguing sounds.

Life at Hyde Park Gardens was divided into three distinct sections; the domestics, who lived in the basement and on the top floor; my Grandmother, who moved sedately in and out of her rooms on the first and second floors; and our rooms which were on the third floor. There were half floors too, which took in my Grandmother's writing room and Father's study.

The stairs were divided into three too. The stone stairs to the basement, then the lovely shallow wide stairs thickly carpeted to the very edge. Here and there in the corners were statues of ladies in draped garments holding aloft lamps. We took the shallow stairs two at a time negotiating the corners so as not to collide with these 'ladies of the lamp'. When it came to passing Father's door, you doubled your pace in case he called out for you to come in. When we were small Mother used to dispense coconut candy of white and pink slabs to us in this little room. Father took little notice of us. But as we grew up, he would call us in for a talk or a little prayer. Once he manoeuvred us all together and when Pauline would not do her turn at praying aloud we all reached out with our legs to kick her, because we wanted to be finished and gone. But Pauline, after a long silence, won the round, and Father said, as we got up, 'Well, Pauline, you seem to have nothing to ask God for. You must be a millionaire.'

On Granny's bedroom floor, you could look over the bannisters to a drop of two floors sheer down to where the gong stood. Here the fun was to have a shot at spitting on to Ryall's head as he rang the gong, until he reported us to Granny!

The third flight of stairs led to our portion of the

house; they were steeper and the carpets were thinner. You could feel the freedom coming on you as you mounted. Very free it was up there. After your bath you ran the length of the passage naked without being caught by anyone coming up the back stairs and arrived dripping in the bedroom to dry before the fire.

Three of us slept in a large room overlooking the street, undressing by the fire on winter's nights, discussing the day. We then went to sleep, slowly and drowsily, talking and watching the bobbles bordering the mantel shadowed against the ceiling in the firelight.

Mother's room was sunny and overlooked the gardens; the windows were wide and her ivory brushes would be seen drying in the sun on the sill. Once, one fell smashing to the terrace far below and there was only one left. In summer time the daisies on the lawns were thick, and we would get Ryall to give us the key and go down and sit among them and make daisy chains. Often Father invaded our precincts and, standing in Mother's room, he would practise a straight stroke in front of her long glass with his cricket bat. Mother was easy, she knew everything and understood. She even managed Father to a certain extent. It was 'Charlie this', and 'Charlie that', and 'No Charlie! Oh, Charlie!' I think these were the happiest days of my parents' lives and it had the effect of making us feel cosy and secure.

Grandmother's sister, Aunt Hannah, lived at 32 Gloucester Square and had an establishment run on the same lines as Granny's, except that instead of a parrot she owned a black Pomeranian dog with strange upstanding ears, called Impy. Impy had a disquieting way of flying to the attack when you entered the drawing-room with loud yappings, and Aunt Hannah's voice crackling behind in protest.

We would often lunch with her on Sundays, two by

two. This was popular as we had ginger beer for lunch and usually came away with a tip of a gold sovereign each. Aunt Hannah was very deaf. Kyte, her large imposing butler, would shout in her left ear the name of the dish; Aunt Hannah, because she was deaf in this ear, would turn her head the other way to reply, whereupon Kyte would slip round the other side to repeat it; then she, not knowing which side he was on, would turn again. This game amused us greatly and we were always suspicious that Kyte put it on to make us laugh.

Here too, in her large formal house, long french windows opened on to a terrace and lawns with shady trees. In summer time there was an air of cricket and trailing flimsy frocks, leg o'mutton sleeves, hats perched forward, and strawberries and cream.

There were comings and goings between the butlers of both houses. Aunt Hannah would send a specially good cake or tartlet to Granny, and Granny return the favour later in the week. The butlers would consort together, exchanging the family news. Then one day a most serious message came for my Father and Mother to come and stay with Aunt Hannah as Impy was very ill. When he died Father had to arrange for his burial, and he was solemnly packed on the kitchen table in a shoe box, with the whole staff standing round. Suddenly a long agonized squawk rent the silence. (My Father had stepped back on the cat's tail.) This had an electric effect on one and all, who thought that Impy had come back to life in his very coffin, making the maids scream with horror. When they eventually recovered, everyone nearly laughed, till they remembered the solemn occasion.

Those were the days when Christmas had a magic thrill. The German band would wake us at midnight, playing 'Hark the Herald Angels', and moving your feet to the end of the bed you could feel that Santa Claus had not forgotten.

How can I ever forget those Christmases? The round table with tablecloth to the floor, shiny with ironed starch, the glitter of silver and glass, the food out of this world. We would weigh each other before and after Christmas lunch and Cousin Vera, aged five, was found to have put on five pounds, at which her brother Bernard was accused of having put his foot on the scales.

Coming down to the dining-room one such evening before tea, with no one in sight, I saw the enormous Christmas cake, black inside, with almond and sugar icing. It stood on the revolving 'dumb waiter' in the middle of the table, surrounded by finely cut sandwiches and sweetly coloured cakes. An enormous silver tray opposite Grandmother's chair held the lavender-coloured cups and saucers with gold handles; and a space was left for the heavy silver tea-pot and water-jug. With a quick look round the doors of the room, I sliced myself a stupendous door-step of the Christmas cake. Its dimensions were such as I had never before seen in anybody's hand. Lying down on the sofa so as to gain more strength for the task, I demolished the whole lot before anyone appeared. I have often wondered since if the poor quality of my digestion took shape from that heavenly quarter of an hour.

It must have been about 1896 and our ages ranged from four to ten years, when we came to Matcham Farm for a holiday and Father played in a series of cricket matches on Lord Harris' estate nearby.

One evening there was great excitement in the candle-lit rooms upstairs. Father and Mother were to dine at the Harrises. We ran from room to room in our nightdresses watching, first Father putting in his cuff-links, then Mother doing her hair. Finally, when all was ready, we leaned out of the window to pipe in chorus, 'Goodbye, Goodbye.' At the white gate they paused to wave farewell. On the light evening air a blue ribbon fluttered from my mother's waist. Was it that ribbon that started a worldly desire in my small bosom, that was perhaps never to be extinguished? A few days after I came upon a big blue bead. I followed everyone about the house to find something with which to tie it to the third finger of my left hand. At last a piece of wool was found. At lunch I became confused because I knew Father would not approve. I worked quickly under the table to turn the bead to the underside of my finger. It would not budge. At last came Father's voice. 'Edith, here is your plate.' I turned my hand upwards to receive it, hiding the bead. He spotted this at once and announced, 'So we have a Jezebel among us.' There was a horrified silence. Then he said, 'You know what happens to Jezebels? They get thrown out of the window.' Whereupon, he carried me to the low window and toppled me out on to the grass. There I crouched by the wall for what seemed like hours till eventually Mother found me, and in her arms I slowly realized that perhaps it was not after all a crime to wear a blue bead ring.

There was the day Father had us all rigged up with dark blue bloomers made by a local dressmaker, and in this get-up we learnt to ride bicycles. This was fun, but the *dénouement* came with the day we were taken on the public roads, Father leading the way looking back over his shoulder with some disappointment at the three small bloomer-clad girls struggling not only with the ride uphill but with the sense of the indignity of the whole show.

His efforts to teach us cricket, to be photographers, to ride, made me begin to wonder if it were not his effort to turn us all into boys.

4

INDIAN SUMMER—1900

THOREAU said, 'If a man does not keep in step with his fellows, it may be because he hears a different drummer.' Father was like that; he was not a man to join one particular Church—he believed in any Church or community who 'loved Jesus Christ in sincerity'. When in 1895 he returned from China, and was considering his next departure, the whole family tried to persuade him to join the Church of England, but he dug in his heels. The argument raged so strongly that it came to a head-on clash with his brother Herbert and his wife, as they sat round the dining-room table after dinner one evening. The shaded candles and heavy red curtains, reaching from ceiling to floor, made a comfortable surround to this most uncomfortable skirmish, and I fled upstairs.

In 1900 Father left for South India to minister to the Union Church in Ootacamund, which was evangelical and of no special denomination and was attended mostly by the Ango-Indian community. We four girls and Mother followed him amid a bewildering array of boxes, domed trunks and all the other accoutrements of family travel.

On the steamer going to India, our ages ranging from twelve to six years, we were already becoming conscious of dress and our effect on the young ship's officers—or rather I should say their effect on us! In order of age, there was first Grace, the anxious leader for ever terrified as to what the next two would be up to; Dorothy and myself always quarrelling, she the socialite, and I the swaggerer; then, bringing up the rear, small but bold Pauline, the policeman, who was for ever saying, 'If you don't stop, I'll send a chit to Mother!'

To the small edifice, known locally as the Tin Tabernacle, came all sorts and sundry. Sometimes one of the A.D.C.s from Government House would be seen in the back row. The choir was composed of deep-bosomed, contralto ladies, singing Sankey hymns, with double chins brought in to fill the bag of sound.

Colonel and Mrs. Stevenson, old as our Grandmother, were the guiding lights. We sat with them in the same pew on Sundays. As we grew restless, they did their best to suppress our activities. One day prowling round the empty church—Father in the vestry probably arranging about the weekly social—I climbed into the pulpit and found printed by hand on a large card, 'Please to remember the limit of time.' I settled at once on Colonel Stevenson as the audacious printer trying to control Father's lengthy sermons.

Another time, my curiosity knowing no bounds, I was caught by the 'Peun' (the Indian church-warden) just lifting the lid of the polished mahogany box that held the Communion wine. I posed this question to myself during one of the long sermons, 'What did communion wine taste like?' One day I accosted Father and said, 'I think we are old enough now to take Communion.' He was delighted, and we were all questioned as to our beliefs. We must have given satisfactory answers, for soon he was preparing a large tin lining of a packing case in the garden which he let into the ground. I remember thinking that I had hardly bargained for this, although to Father it was the next best thing to the River Jordan.

The day arrived, pouring with rain, the whole Tin Tabernacle congregation assembling under umbrellas to sing around the baptismal tank. Clad in nightdresses, we were totally immersed in this same tank. At this unusual performance even Father got confused and named two of us wrong. But his methods certainly left their impression. Years later when I went to Sherborne School, I was asked if I would like to be confirmed and I said, 'Certainly not. I have already been baptized by my Father—I do not think anything more is needed.' This so disconcerted my house mistress that I was sent to the Head, Miss Mulliner, and evidently also confounded that great lady, for no more was said.

This Indian summer, which lasted five and a half years, was our happiest childhood. There were picnics, badminton parties, outings with the young A.D.C.s of Government House, morning rides two by two with Father. Ootacamund was a very social place where the Regiments, settled in the plains of Madras, came up for leave in the lovely hill country.

Father was keen that we should excel at outdoor sports, and, although we showed little inclination or aptitude, he did his best to make riders out of us. I went to him one day and said, 'I am looking forward to my ride tomorrow morning.' I knew it would please him, but I was absolutely terrified for we rode untrained native ponies. Their delight was to gallop around the gymkhana with us on their backs, then suddenly stop and kick up their heels sending us shooting over their heads. Father did not help matters by riding behind us on his large Australian waler with a cart whip in his hand. The crack kept us moving at a good pace. We had no riding clothes and our skirts would fly up showing our bloomers. This filled us with shame, especially when we met some of the young officers riding, so we safety-pinned our skirts to the saddle in front. These mercifully gave way when we took a toss. Dorothy was the only real horsewoman among us; she seemed to be able to handle anything she rode.

Father's cricket, long ago laid aside when he went to China, now came into play again. There were matches every week in the centre of the gymkhana. When the game was over he would bring the young officers back with him to stay for the night. In the morning you often found a sleeping figure on the sitting-room divan, which faced us with the question as to whether to do our practice at the piano or make the very good excuse of not waking the visitor.

The days went by quickly, days of monsoon, days of brilliant sunshine, at an altitude of 8,000 feet. The air acted like a pep pill and no escapade seemed impossible. Father would put all four of us into a buggy cart and, with Billie the waler harnessed, would take us up the most stupendous hills with cobble stones and down the other side, while we hung on like grim death. Billie entered into all this with Father's same sense of humour, arching his neck and throwing out his forelegs to tackle with a will anything Father set him to. When we arrived at the house my Mother, having sensed that we had come the short cut, would cry, 'Oh, Charlie this,' and 'Oh, Charlie that.'

A happy childhood is like standing under the sun—there are no shadows, you live in the present with all the enthusiasm of your young heart. The past is past; as for the future, it will be as it always is. There was only one thing that marred my days in India, and that was a creeping sense of fear. When it was let slip by one of the grown-ups that a tiger had been seen in the blue gum forest above our house, just where we had been playing that very afternoon, I did not know how to contend with this fear. Instead of telling someone, I bawled my head off and nobody could imagine what was wrong with me. Our excellent cook was another worry. He would get drunk and chase the other boys around the kitchen table with a carving knife, and then shouting his grievances would set to and make the most delicate and delicious pancakes and meringues. There came the night when our pet rabbits were stolen from outside our french window. Next morning a long knife was found on top of the box. I shivered and prayed that Mother, who slept next door, would leave her door open at night.

The other sisters showed no signs of these secret fears. We slept three or four in a row, and the nights were made glamorous by evening parties. Sitting up in bed, our nightdresses folded back at the neck and a piece of lace tucked in at the throat for effect, we would produce the cakes and sweets we had smuggled into our laps at children's parties. Each of us would take the name of someone we knew, balancing these trophies on a piece of paper we handed them round and, in a very social voice, would say, 'Lady A, will you take a little curry and rice?' Pauline, aged six, to whom we had assigned a husband from the Tin Tabernacle, a bespectacled and freckled young man with a rather sugary manner, would be asked, 'And how is your husband today?' I remember Pauline getting up and stamping on the floor, 'I won't have him! I won't have him!' We dived under the clothes to stifle our shouts of laughter.

Our favourite among the officers was a Captain Crookenden, who would bring his polo ponies to Ootacamund with him and allow us to ride them. This was a welcome change from the 'tat' ponies. Dorothy, as plump and juicy as a loquat, soon became his favourite, earning the endearing nickname of Topsy; in retaliation I must have done some grim things, so he nicknamed me 'Satan'.

After five years some of us were showing signs of the high altitude. We had nearly driven three governesses nuts, learning nothing ourselves but probably teaching them a thing or two. This made the parents turn their eyes once again towards home and proper schooling. It must have been 1906 that we sailed away, our skirts a little longer, our sense of the world around us sharpened, and an excitement to live as we had never lived before.

5

GEESE OR SWANS

OUR excitement soon died down. We came back to a short-lived stay at Hyde Park Gardens, in preparation for going to school in Switzerland. We approached this new plan somewhat guardedly. The day came in the autumn of 1906 for three of us to leave for Lausanne, because Pauline was too young for this school. Mother saw us off at Victoria. We knew she loved us but seldom showed us any outward affection. But that day I saw, as the train moved out, a tear in her eye. I felt moved beyond words. She would miss us—she who never thought her geese were swans—she cared. I sank back in my seat to realize how little love I had shown her, how small a gratitude we gave in return for all she did for us. She must have had her heartaches, but she never spoke of them. Now, there was no more time. I longed to fly back and say, 'Darling Mother, thank you.' Instead the thought stuck in my heart, 'Too late.'

Arrived at Lausanne, we three were put to sleep in a room together overlooking Caux. At dark, away in the distance you could see the lights of the hotel like a glittering jewel on the hillside.

We were told to speak only French. We disregarded all rules and spoke English. We were reported. Indeed before many months were out, we were in real hot water and up before the headmistress for participating in a circular of articles written by some of the upper girls, with comic and crude descriptions of the staff and their ways. I had copied them out of an exercise book marked PRIVAT. My book was found, I was confronted with it and the unanswerable question, 'Qu'est que c'est ce PRIVAT?' Authority was outraged. Something had to be done. A dozen of us were threatened with expulsion, but we were let off with a caution in the end.

Here it was that my first show of being a born shopkeeper revealed itself. I could hardly believe my luck one Sunday when I managed to swop my weekly packet of chocolate with a girl for her white fox fur which I admired. Not long after the fur changed hands again to another girl who willingly gave me quite a valuable brooch in exchange. Years after in a moment of conscience I returned it, saying it was not a fair bargain. Imagine my chagrin when, by return, she wrote that she had sold it to the nearest jeweller as she had never liked it herself.

Days went by when we attempted to become good scholars—it was a hard grind and we were often homesick. One evening, practising the piano in the twilight, I put my head down on the keys and longed and longed, not for any person or thing, but just a sound—the clip-clop of a hansom cab trotting down Bayswater Road. The days went by slowly until, in eighteen months' time, speaking rather poor French, we returned to Hyde Park Gardens and were sent to Sherborne School. Dorothy and I arrived feeling ourselves to be much-travelled misses. Born in China, home to England, five years in India, followed by one and a half in Switzerland, and now Sherborne. But Sherborne thought nothing of it. Could we play cricket? was the first question asked of us. We were soon to show them that we couldn't. These years were spent equally unsuccessfully as regards our education. We simply 'did not know how to use our brains,' so the mistresses said. 'The brains are there, but too many governesses is the trouble.' And after an uneventful two years, leaving from the form known as the 'Waste Paper Basket', we returned once more to London.

Back at Hyde Park Gardens there were sunny days in July when tickets were to be had for the Oxford and Cambridge, and Eton and Harrow, cricket matches.

On the Thursday in between the matches, Granny always had her big at home day. Dressed in our expensive looking outfits given us by Granny, we would look forward with excitement to the festive occasion. A snapshot taken on the terrace on such a morning shows a young girl in a grey corded coat and skirt. The coat is caught in at the waist, the skirt goes to the ground. The clumsy bunch of material caught at one knee shows it did not come from the very best shop. The hair is an attempt at sobriety, smoothed to the cheeks; the face reveals a world of doubt.

I wondered about my sisters, but for myself only half of me belonged to the life of Hyde Park Gardens. The other half felt guilty that I did not follow my parents, who had renounced their former gay life and become missionaries. Secretly I felt at war in myself, undecided, reluctant to throw in my lot with them, yet I felt a stranger to the world that was shouting its welcome.

Perhaps to cover up the missionary stamp on us we bought hats that were large as cartwheels, clothes just too loud, colours too bright—so that one of our uncles warned his daughters, 'Those Charlie Studd girls are fast.' And poor Father groaned when he took us out, because, being a missionary, it was not seemly to have such daughters. Aunt Mary, whose husband was 'our Coldstream uncle',[1] tried to guide our taste in clothes. Of those velvet hats with a small ostrich feather tucked under the brim at the side, she said firmly 'I should remove the feather.'

1. Brigadier H. W. Studd, D.S.O., Coldstream Guards.

As to jewellery, we could never pass a shop without flattening our noses against the windows. Before long we made ways and means of possessing what we wanted. Dorothy and I were sent off to do typing and shorthand at the Polytechnic, with ten shillings each for lunches for the week. We saved out of this and there came the day when Dorothy acquired a synthetic ruby ring. But how was she to account for it? Her contrivance was to post it to herself with a card inside, 'From an unknown admirer'.

In these days I fought my first battle with myself. Dorothy had a peach-like complexion. I was inclined to be pale. There came the day when I bought my first tiny paper packet of rouge. You licked the little paper and rubbed it on your cheeks. But my conscience played such havoc with me that I alternately rubbed it off and on as the battle waged one way then the other. So that some days Granny would say, 'You do look well,' and on others, 'How pale you are.'

Then again Dorothy was always the favourite, anyway with the boys. I felt life was not worth living unless I could gain the same attention. How to do it? Owing to constant jealousies between us we were often at loggerheads. Obviously the thing was to learn from her her source of secret power. In a boat on the lake at Uncle Sky Thomas's I asked her to be my friend and help me. She told me many home truths, very kindly, how I showed off and threw my weight about too much. What to do and not to do. This brought me one of the greatest friendships of my life. We became such friends that we swore we would not go away and stay without each other. She taught me much, but I think I learnt most from watching her; she was so natural and sweet, and she had the gift of running to fulfil your merest wish with a gaiety that made everything such fun.

Our playmates were four boy cousins who lived in Harley Street. They were all just older than we were, so that it often turned to playing families. Each boy paired off with the opposite girl, except that Lionel never liked me so that Dorothy always ended up with two husbands and me with none. So much did this game persist that when we grew older both parents felt it their duty to warn their children they could not marry cousins. The baldness of this warning struck us all as so crude that when we next met we were filled with smouldering anger and we all sat glaring at each other in silence.

Meanwhile (in the few months we were in London) we came to love every aspect of our small lives. The family house gathered you up like loving arms—the uncles, aunts and cousins. There must have been at least forty of the family who came and went regularly. The large L-shaped drawing-room softly lit by whispering gas; rose curtains of stiff damask silk drawn close; the flashing fire in the grate; my Grandmother in her close-fitting black silk, rustling as she walked between her guests, breathing in short little gasps, stay-bones, silk, all working with their small sounds as she progressed. I can see Aunt Mary, tall and graceful, standing in a pool of light made by the fire, clad in a flimsy dress of flowing red chiffon. With her white hair, and her young and beautiful face, she looked a dream of loveliness. She had exceptionally large blue eyes which we used to refer to with wonder as 'Aunt Mary's gooseberry eyes'. She stood talking with a charm and gaiety which made her my guiding star in all matters of how to behave and what to wear. I learned from her that simplicity in dress was the thing, rather than fussy decoration. Her daughters, Mary and Do, about our own age, filled us with admiration, because they were so bold, and always laughed with their mouths wide open, were always turned out in neat and well-cut coats and skirts and felt hats with the Brigade colours. How we envied them!

We had come to love the sounds of London—the muffin man with his bell on a Tuesday evening; the roll of the growler, and the smart clip-clop of the hansom cab spanking down Bayswater Road; the barrel organ twanging out some old song which would touch your heart with melancholy; the shouts of newspaper boys; the steps of the lamplighter; the silence of the streets at midnight. Then there were the more intimate sounds about the house—the soft jingle of glass and silver coming up in the lift to the dining-room, the to-ing and fro-ing of the footman laying the table, the door-bell ringing clear down below, and charging steps coming up the back stairs to answer it, the tinkling of spoons in saucers at teatime, the chimes of the clock over the dining-room door, the boom of the gong, three great crashes and a rattle of drums dying away in the house. The uncles and aunts and cousins, revolving always around the dignified figure of my Grandmother gave us a sense of secure family life, while the arrival of fresh people produced an unusual shyness in us, sometimes amounting to a feeling of overpowering inadequacy to meet the occasion.

I recall one Saturday. Distant cousins from Wales arrived for lunch. Uncle George was on a visit from the U.S.A. and I was the only one of the sisters at home. One could always shelter behind Granny's complete command of any situation. But with these young men, so immaculate, sophisticated, handsome, and with an air of distinction—they looked like racehorses—I felt isolated and afraid. They looked at me with sly amusement: 'One of Uncle Charlie's daughters, no doubt!' I was flattered when Uncle George asked me to join them and go to Lords for the afternoon. I spent that wonderful summer day basking like a small fish among the big fry, so overwhelmed with the effect of the young men that I came home eventually to collapse in tears in my room. I could not tell why; perhaps because we had never had a brother. Hugh married eventually and went to Paris as Councillor to the British Embassy—he was killed when about forty years old, riding one of his own horses in training for the Derby. Bill went out to the family tea firm in Calcutta, to be caught up in the war of 1914–18 and he died on a battlefield in France. But that day they had a godlike quality that struck me like a flash of light from another world.

6

THE ONLY DUKE

As we know, the years leading up to the first World War marked the end of a brilliant decade. They were days of security, the stamp of the seasons as sure as a postage stamp on an envelope. In summer it was luncheon at 1.45, the carriage at the front door at 3 p.m., calling with Granny on her friends, cards handed in, waiting outside while she visited, sometimes being invited in myself to a plate of strawberries and cream. The window boxes would vie with each other all down the street. It was the time of cricket matches, sometimes a visit to Eton, large hats, lace umbrellas, night parties; so warm that you could stand in your nightdress and watch the balcony of Clarendon Place opposite fill with ladies in lovely evening dresses and men in white ties, their laughter floating on the sultry air.

On such a summer's day it must have been, that, ever ambitious and pushing, I approached my Grandmother. 'Granny,' I said, 'I don't know a duke. Could you introduce me to one?' (I did not tell her that it had been murmured in the servants' hall, 'You see, Miss Edith will marry a duke.') Granny was amused. 'Very well,' she said, 'we will go together to the Duchess of Somerset's "At Home" next week.'

On the morning of the great day, I trotted down Oxford Street and bought myself a veil with spots both large and small on it, as I felt befitted the occasion. In a hat with a feather of no great pretension, and the veil firmly knotted under my chin, we started off together. The big house with its semi-circular staircase rising out of a large hall, the liveried servants, the flower decoration, soft carpets and music, filled me with the magnitude of the occasion. I summoned all my powers, both social and conversational. Stepping behind my Grandmother, with her faintly rustling figure, we mounted the stairs and entered an enormous room full of people. The stentorian announcement, 'Mrs. Studd and Miss Studd', gave one the sense that this was a golden opportunity.

I think there must have been some collaboration, for soon the Duke was found. That he was bald, tall and had a corpulent figure did not matter at all. I gazed up at him in awe, as he no doubt began with, 'Well, and how's your Father?' At this psychological moment a plate of sponge fingers was handed to me; I took one, and put it straight into my veiled mouth. Looking up at my one and only Duke in dismay, I had to extricate it from my now crumby veil, undoing the knot while he gallantly held my cup without showing a flicker of amusement.

There came times when we all became too much for Granny and were sent off for long spells in a small house in Bedford, and another time to a house at Barnet, which we christened the Bunny Hutch.

It was at the Bunny Hutch that my sister, Dorothy, began to receive many letters from Gilbert, and wrestled with herself, both alone and in company with his sister, as to whether she was in love. I was kept out of this and began to know something of the joy of reading. The life of that saint Madame de la Mothe Guyon fell to me somehow and I tried out my first discipline on myself by refusing at tea time my Mother's then famous coffee cake. This discipline was short lived, for next day I was in to the coffee cake again.

Dorothy was eventually married from Hyde Park Gardens and we returned there for the occasion. The last night came and we slept together in the fourposter in the spare bedroom on Granny's floor. We had been such good friends, but there had been creeping in a strangeness; there was so much she could not share with me now. I remember we read together a little book of devotions and that I wanted so much to cry. This persisted even to the church, where I only kept myself together through the vanity of being chief bridesmaid.

Grace married a year after Dorothy. They went off with discreet trousseaux paid for by Granny's generous gifts and the £40 they had each saved over the years, and £1 each in their purses from Mother. We had been brought up to wear simple underwear with the least of trimming. My envy of Dorothy knew no bounds when I found that she had ribbons run through her chemises and drawers.

Grace married a kind of old man. There is a picture still of the bride, bridesmaids, parents and grandmother taken in the garden of Hyde Park Gardens on the morning of her wedding. The terraced houses stretch in a long row behind us. Grace sits in the middle, her neat face and frame of dark hair enveloped in a frothy veil, her small nose and curling mouth with teeth which always reminded me of beautiful blanched almonds. The older ladies wore velvet. Mother's was mushroom in colour with a high hat. Granny was in satin trimmed with lace, and a lofty bonnet on which I can count five diamond stars.

As for Father, it was one of the few occasions when he could be cajoled into tails. Much of the persuading went on in his dressing-room. The butler, Ryall, was the conjuror.

'Now then, Mr. Charles, we must get this on,' couched in tones of sympathy and he would pull the shirt over

Father's head. A tight fit it was too, over a red flannel waistcoat affair underneath.

'It is so cold,' Father would complain, while Ryall would tell him of his son, a small boy who sang in a church choir—'and little saints they look, sir, with their eyes turned up to heaven. But you and I know what little devils they really are.' At this Father and Ryall would chortle, and sure enough the trousers and coat would be on before Father realized.

Grace went to live in a beautiful house overlooking the Thames. It was a low white house, only two storeys, with numerous tall pillars flanking the front door. At night when the blinds were drawn, red blinds on the first floor, green on the second, with light shining through, it looked like a neapolitan ice cream. The thick soft carpets, blazing fires in every room, the comfort and luxury surrounded us with a cosy security. We loved staying with Grace and Martin. Those cream eggs we had for breakfast, topped with chopped chives; game in wine sauce; junkets covered with thick cream, topped with a deep layer of powdered cinnamon—these were some of the fabulous dishes to be had at Wargrave Manor.

Grace was good to us. The eldest sister, always protecting us, and if need be taking the blame, she now set about to give the remaining two, Pauline and myself, a good time. I remember a weekend at the Ritz. The moments fixed in my memory were lying in a marvellous bath in a green mosaic bathroom suffused with pink lights backed by any number of mirrors. Then there were the flowers, ordered by her husband for the spacious living-room overlooking Piccadilly; and the reflection of Grace in a looking glass, her softly feathered hat and marvellous sables, and the awe-inspiring thought running through my head—indeed the fact—that Grace had an immense sum a year as pocket money, besides all her clothes paid for, and a car and chauffeur of her own.

There was a trip to Brussels. The hotel faced the square with a statue of Godfrey de Bouillon on a rampant horse and at a side window I could hang out and watch the palace guard below. There was some exhibition on where, from a fabulous glass case full of sham pearls I bought, with Grace's approval, a chain not too big in size.

I was secretly gratified that my sisters were safely married. It had been said in our hearing at Hyde Park Gardens—two old heads nodding in concern for us—'What will happen to these girls? They have no money, no one will want to marry them.' To Grace and Pauline this no doubt came as a disconcerting fact to ruminate discreetly in private. But Dorothy and I would roll our eyes like war horses going into battle and would plot and plan to acquit ourselves well in an ordeal that would take all the inspiration and heaven-born genius with which we felt we were endowed. All the same when I came to find myself ensconced at Hyde Park Gardens keeping Granny company by myself I began to feel lonely for younger friends. I had had few and short-lived brushes with the opposite sex, nor was I willing to fall for anybody. There had been the doctor's son at Sherborne School who, seeing my powers on the hockey field one Saturday afternoon, went home and sent me a box of chocolates. It was as large a box as I had ever seen, and I was promptly sent for by the head of the House. Miss Martin and the matron looked at me over their spectacles.

'Edith, do you know anything about this?'

My voice high with panic, I said, 'I have only seen the doctor's son once, and I never even looked at him!'

It was the truth and they accepted it. I was not to acknowledge the chocolates they said, and the box must of course be sent back immediately. They would see to it.

The matter never crossed my mind again until about a year later I was asked by matron to turn out a cupboard in her sanctum. There was the chocolate box, but empty!

Then I received one day towards the end of my schooling a letter, out of which fell a piece of white heather. It was a charming friendly letter from a young man I had met in Scotland, asking me to write to him. Whether it was the Aldershot postmark or what, I never found out. But I was soon on the carpet again, and made to give up the letter and promise not to reply. Some years after the 1914–18 war was over his sister showed me the last photo taken of him. He stands in khaki on Calais docks facing his men. He marched away never to return.

It must have been on a summer's day in 1910 that I prepared to leave Hyde Park Gardens on my first visit alone. My trunk packed, I strolled down the staircase in my mustard and pepper suit feeling just the thing. Cousin Bernard was going to stay at Graham Park near the Hall where I was staying so we were to travel together. The wide dining-room door was open, the terrace beyond basking in sunshine, and the Big Ben chimes over the door, silvery and low, struck one forty-five.

Certain aspects of that day and those to follow remain for ever in my mind. The five mile drive in a car sent to meet me, the long avenue leading up to the house. The huge front door opened into a panelled hall, with paintings of red-coated ancestors hung high over the panelling, and from which a wide dark oak staircase rose to the first floor. I was met by a lady clad in neat black who turned out to be the housekeeper. She led me up to a delightful room with rush carpeting on the floor, and wide open windows looking out on the garden, and miles of fields and woods beyond.

I had met my hostess once before at my sister Dorothy's

wedding. At the reception she had asked me to go and stay with her and I was given to understand by those who knew that this was a singular compliment. The most fitting description of her I came across in a few lines I found the other day:

The gracious calm and stately mien
Of movements full of grace and power
The eyes, the looks, the gait of Queens.

After tea together, the two daughters and I went to play clock golf with some man friend staying there. When my turn came to play I saw out of the corner of my eye two figures descend the stone steps from one side of the house. They strolled over to us. After very perfunctory bows and how-do-you-dos from these two men, I applied myself to my stroke. But I was shaken to the core, for Anthony had all the grace and power of his mother. And in the presence of one who had such a sudden and profound effect on me, how could I play my turn in my mustard and pepper suit which, in that instant, I felt was all wrong?

Day after day my feelings of inadequacy gained on me. I fell every hour under the magnetic spell of this silent young man, the son of the house. He took no notice of me; he scarcely troubled to look at me. But in the evening when the men played billiards, I would sit by the fire and watch this perfect figure of a man, with his prematurely greying hair. How wide was the gulf between him and me! This family moved in what my parents would have called 'a worldly circle'. They lived for riding; indeed they could ride any horse, anyhow, anywhere. There were polo matches, point to points, when Anthony would often win the race. There were dances, which we had never been allowed to attend as dancing was considered to be worldly by my parents and so I stayed behind like some Cinderella. I found myself more and more making my way up to the schoolroom to sit with the two daughters where, among other matters, they would discuss the kind of men they were going to marry. This was too near the point for me, and I kept silent. Or I would join my hostess in the high mullioned window, where she would sit like some medieval figure embroidering immense curtains, her head bent like an exotic flower, her hands like pale butterflies moving over the work, and I would listen to her talking.

At the end of the visit I fled to Dorothy who was living with her husband in the north of England. Here in her friendly presence I was able to pour out my anguish for a love that was not returned. I would write to him I said; I would tell him that though I was poor I loved him dearly. To this indiscreet, undignified, indeed wild, idea, she listened in shocked silence. Then my brother-in-law stepped in and, like a black cloth covering the magic, he gave advice in no uncertain voice. I could not do it, he said. I must not do it.

Looking back over the years I came to realize later, strange as it may seem, that pain could be worked into the tapestry of my life in such rich colours. I had been in love and had experienced the complete outgoing of one person towards another. In its unfulfilment I had known a kind of death, yet in loving I had also gained a reward.

7

ALFRED

MY Father now had another inspiration, combined with the determination necessary, to go out to Central Africa and start mission work in the Upper Congo. His friend, Karl Kumm, who advertised his meetings with a poster outside announcing, 'Cannibals want missionaries', had been speaking all over England on the serious fact that the Mohammedans were sweeping down over Africa, making converts and, unless a chain of mission stations were made across the centre of Africa, nothing would stop them. Karl Kumm was a large man, of German extraction, with a deep melodious voice. Father said he had only to mention the name of one place in Africa in his resonant voice, sounding something like Ouwagawagadoogoo, and all the old ladies in the audience would reach for their handkerchiefs and their purses.

In spite of this joke, there is no doubt that Father himself was deeply stirred and wanted to start the first mission in the middle of this chain, plumb in the heart of Africa. It set my Grandmother crying and my Mother weeping silently on the third floor of Hyde Park Gardens. Her helpless cries of, 'Oh, Charlie, how could you!' were of no avail. He set about speaking everywhere that he could get an opening in order to collect recruits. No money was mentioned. Money came by faith and prayer. No offer of speaking did he turn down. Sometimes it would be in the churches, more often in mission halls no matter how small. It meant he slept anywhere, and on one occasion he found his host was the local fishmonger and under his bed was stored the day's catch of fish. In the morning they washed together under the kitchen tap and shared one towel. It mattered not to him, he drew from his fellow men such warmth and companionship. Soon money came pouring in from rich and poor, sometimes as small as a half-crown postal order.

Uncle Willie Bradshaw was willing to pay for the whole expedition, but on condition that Father saw a doctor. This he did and the doctor turned him down flat. From the time he had typhoid in China, he had suffered from asthma. How could a man in his state of health carry out such a campaign?

Uncle Willie withdrew his offer. Nothing deterred Father. He had heard the call, he must go, no matter the cost. He wrote a pamphlet at this time called 'The Chocolate Soldier', which showed up the flabbiness of Christians. It stirred up antagonism as well as inspiration. His great saying was, 'If Jesus Christ be God and died for me, no sacrifice can be too great for me to make for Him.' When it came to speaking to the Universities, his message brought forth a mixed reception. Speaking in the Guildhall, Cambridge, (it must have been about 1911) to a packed audience, the front rows crowded with Dons to whom he was still the great cricketer, he spoke on his 'Chocolate Soldier' message. At the end of the meeting the Dons filed out in silent disapproval. But the undergraduates were intrigued with his audacity and soon there was a request for him to come and speak to them only. Again the Guildhall was packed. They listened attentively to his challenging message, not without a certain uneasiness at the call that they should go out to Africa with no special financial support. Their faith was to be in a God who would supply their every need. Father sensed their reluctance and ended with this: 'No need to tell me what you are thinking. You are saying, "Here am I, Lord, but send my sister." '

There were some twenty-four who tentatively answered the call. Less than half found their way to missionary work in Africa.

To me my Father's goings on were quite incomprehensible. As a family we had had enough adversity. To go out and seek more was sheer madness. But his life and message must have reached my subconscious; for when it came for me to go to Africa for a much lesser motive, I found myself able to do so. There is no doubt that he was a man of extraordinary vision and compelling presence. His messages were charged with challenge, humour and emotion. But it was his realism in living out his own message that attracted those who were looking for sincerity in a world of fashionable poses.

A contemporary of Father's was his friend, Barclay Buxton. He was a big powerful man with red hair and a healthy complexion, known to his Cambridge friends as 'Beef'. Like my Father, he had been nurtured in the lap of luxury. He had gone out to Japan and established a mission, spending his own money freely and supporting it for years afterwards. With his wife and four small boys he left his home, Easneye in Hertfordshire, annexing his father's estate carpenter and two housemaids to go with them. These two gallant ladies became great stalwarts in the Japan Band, as the mission was called.

The second of his sons, Alfred, was up at Cambridge in 1910, studying to become a doctor. He was tall and light of build, red-haired like his father, with the truest of grey eyes that looked straight at you. He heard my Father speak and, after careful thought and with great courage, threw up his doctoring—by this time he had passed his second M.B.—and offered to accompany Father on his next journey to Africa. Naturally this caused a hue and cry from the Buxton family who said how unwise it was to go with this 'hare-brained man' as some called him. Alfred was sent round to receive the advice of many missions and medical men. Ultimately he was left alone with his decision, and in the end his Father, who was a great man in more ways than one, consented to let him go.

Alfred was an ideal companion for Father. It was not only what they had in common, but that they were complementary to each other. Father was a soldier, often regimenting his missionaries to their great discomfort; Alfred was a Quaker at heart, peace-loving, and able to see the other side of a position. I heard my Father once say, 'All very well, Alfred, but I can't *afford* to see the other side.'

They were alike in their sincerity. They were both completely committed to God, and it did not matter what happened to themselves. I never saw either of them fear anything or any man. Alfred was the only person in my life who helped me to understand and appreciate my own Father. It could indeed be said of them that 'they had that true courage which is shown by performing without witnesses, that which one would do before the whole world'.

Alfred and I met in 1910 when my parents had taken us four girls to stay with Father's old friend, Barclay Buxton. The four boys were there, we were all more or less the same ages, and soon made friends. We spent a delectable week playing tennis, canoeing on a pond, potting at rocks with a gun, and visiting their grandparents' home, Easneye, two miles over the fields. We left the Buxtons and went to stay with Aunt Dora Bradshaw, and from that time Alfred (the second son) and I began to write to each other. I shall never forget the arrival of his first letter, brought in by a crisp housemaid on the early morning tea-tray. We had been such good friends that I had tossed up each morning, would he write or not? Sure enough on the third morning there was his first letter. For two years we wrote to each other and met as occasion allowed. Then I began to feel that I knew so few men and still needed to be free, and I remembered that Mother had said not to marry the first man who asked me. I wrote my feelings to Alfred. I was in Scotland at a house party for the 12th when the reply came. It was steady and devoted, as he had always been. For him nothing was changed. I was right to be free. But should I ever want to come back he would always be waiting. Two years were to pass before we met again.

At the end of 1913 the time came for them to sail. There was to be a farewell meeting at which Father and Alfred were to speak. Quite a number of the family were present. Father spoke with his usual aplomb and zest. The difficulties were great but he 'didn't care a brass button'. This had become quite a well-known saying of Father's. A small cousin, Charlie Bradshaw, leaned forward at this and looked at me down the row. In a small voice he piped up. 'There goes Uncle Charlie's brass button again!'

Then came Alfred's turn. He spoke in a quiet and constant manner. He had a quality in him that would serve till the world's end, and be loyal to God's cause to which he felt called. He had a new authority, was far from lacking in humour, and there was added compassion and understanding for others. I sensed this and was drawn to him afresh.

Was this the familiar friend? This man who had been at my side for so long; had he caught up with me at last? All night long, irresolute in heart and will, I sought a clue to end my searchings. With the light of day I rang him up. His voice, strong, warm, confident, had always affected me strangely. I asked him if he would like to come up and see me. He hesitated, for he had only so few days with his parents. I suggested he came up on the afternoon train, and that we met at the bookstall on Liverpool Street Station.

Neither of us gave anything away when we met. A taxi strike was on, but a kind fellow stopped in answer to our hail.

Sitting awkwardly in our corners, I said, 'Do you know why I wanted to see you?'

And he, the wonder dawning on his face, said, 'No!'

And I said, 'Yes!'

The taxi man said, 'You haven't told me where to go.'

We said, 'Drive anywhere!'

At the end of half an hour he shouted back, 'My petrol is giving out. What shall I do?'

We said, 'That tea shop in Victoria! Take us there.'

Amid thick cups and saucers and frightful cakes, while sipping our tea, Alfred suddenly said, 'Come home with me.'

'No, I can't,' I said, 'I haven't got anything with me.'

He said, 'Never mind, come.'

So we caught the next train down to Hertfordshire. We walked up from the station in the dark.

Leaving me on the doorstep, he said, 'I had better go in first and warn them.'

Father Buxton came out and gave me a bear-like hug and brought me in to the warmth of a fire and a home which had always held a welcome for me. That night, in a nightdress borrowed from my future mother-in-law, I sought the quiet of the spare room after a very long day. I looked at myself in the long glass in the aforesaid nightdress. It was of Jaeger flannel, buttoned up to the neck, and only reached to my knees. I took one look at myself and dived into bed.

A few days passed and it was time for Father Buxton

and me to see them off. We went with them as far as Paris. The train left at ten o'clock at night. Few people seemed about. Alfred drew me aside and with the steam from the engine hissing in our ears, he said some words to me. I can remember nothing, except it was our goodbye. When would I see him again? When would it be possible for women to go out where no white woman had ever been? This parting so soon descended like a desolation on my being. I heard him speak in that well-known voice, so warm and reassuring. Through the grey mist we gazed up at them at the carriage window in the panic it is so hard to hide. Leaning out, one too old and one too young, the station lights seemed to turn their faces green. How desperate the futility of ordinary conversation. There was nothing left to be said. The next instant everything was going to stop. The huge train pulled out and they were gone. I felt stifled with the weight of time and the leaden moments ticking away one by one. Of the journey back nothing remains. Only the slow, painful movement forwards and getting back to life.

The days, weeks and months of four years dragged themselves away, so painfully slow those early days, then imperceptibly gaining in momentum until I was again in the swim of my frivolous life, visiting here and there. The future, with any chance of us meeting, was grey indeed. And who can keep up a friendship over years on the thin string of letters which took six weeks to come? There were times when we seemed to lose contact altogether.

It was about the third year of my engagement that I went to stay in Scotland. Strange and mysterious it is that friendship that springs from a fleeting look or touch. From the first moment, John, the son of the house, and I became friends. Alfred was very far away. The days were young days, happy days.

Then my sister and I went on a second visit which was not quite such a success. My brother-in-law had died. In those days everyone went into black on the slightest pretext and I had one of these serious turns I have been addicted to all my life, when any sense of humour I may have seems to desert me. I went to Mother and said, 'Pauline and I can't possibly go and stay at Lockwood Hall unless we have black evening dresses.'

Mother never had much money anyway to play with, I am sure I do not know where she found it. However, money in hand and no advice from her, we were soon off to Debenham's to buy one dress each. I chose two dull black ones to the ground, affairs with large white fichus which crossed over at the back and trailed down in two tails to the hem. 'Exactly like Marie Antoinette,' I thought. A doubt did cross my mind when the assistant referred to them as housecoats, but the drama of looking like Marie Antoinette won the day and off we went with the large box in hand.

We arrived at Lockwood Hall to find a very smart house party in progress and all was most festive. Snow was on the ground, there were lights and roaring fires everywhere. We had tea in the hall, tea as you only find in Scotland, scones of every kind, butter in glass dishes, home-made jams and cakes baked to perfection. Ancestors looked down on us from the walls, some with a shrewd amused look in the eye as if recalling past wonderful teas. In my room that night there was a large hip bath, placed on a rug before the fire. It was delicious to lean back and relax. As the days went by, fun and laughter were everywhere, life was busy and gay. I fell asleep each night in the four-poster with the simple thought, 'How heavenly, there is nothing to do but sleep.' In the morning the maid came in with tea. She was much smarter than I. Indeed, the lady's maid passed me once in the corridor and she looked right through me; a neat little piece in black with a small flimsy white apron. She was patting her hair as if the footman had been kissing her round the corner.

We came down that first evening to find our hostess standing, immaculately dressed, before the drawing-room fire on a huge long-haired white rug. She was swathed in sheer white chiffon to the ground. Her shining hair and flawless complexion, with the blazing fire behind her, made her look like some high priestess before a flaming altar. As Pauline and I advanced down the room like a couple of black mice, I had the terrifying feeling that our Marie Antoinette outfits, the shadow of the guillotine and all that, had misfired. We were definitely underdressed. There is surely nothing more agonizing than dressing up to make an impression and to find in the end you have made the wrong impression. Nothing was said then, but as the evenings went by and we came down again and again in the same sombre attire, my hostess had a few sharp words with me.

'Where are your pretty dresses you wore last time you were here?' she said.

I felt abashed and I did think of sending Mother a wire to post them, but in John's eyes I could do no wrong, so I felt I could get away with it. In fact he laughed like anything and said he did not mind what I had on!

On Sunday we went to the kirk and sat in a wooden pew, which was like a box suspended on the wall. The front was so high you could, if you wanted, snooze away the hours, or suck a peppermint, of which John's father had a supply.

One afternoon when it was pouring with rain, John asked me to go and see the old castle on their estate. Having looked down the oubliette and thrown stones to test how deep it was, and inspected the dungeons, we came up the worn stairs into a large baronial hall. Facing us was a vast fireplace and a coat of arms carved in stone over it. We had always spoken easily together, so here it was, sitting in the mullioned window, on a stone seat flanking the wall, he begged me to drop the idea of going to Africa and to stay and marry him. We were wet and shivering from the rain but the temptation glowed in my heart. How easy to let go of all this going-to-Africa business which seemed so impossible of fulfilment and to say —Yes! How easy to stay and be caught up in this life of grace and ease, and with such an attractive person. His mother was my dear friend, though there were years between us. And a few days before, John's father had caught me in one of the corridors of the house and said, 'Edith, don't go to Africa, I have a nice husband for you.'

To this day I do not know what kept me from saying Yes. I was not strong or noble in character. What was it that kept me back? Torn in two and grief-stricken, my only impulse was to set my foot again on the path I had decided upon and do something positive towards that end.

I travelled south to Mother. I was not going to visit anywhere any more. I must get ready for the future, I told her. If I was to have a child in Africa, I must not be afraid. So I went off to the Salvation Army Mothers' Hospital and worked in the wards for six months, learning all I could. The first baby case I attended in the theatre laid me low on the floor. I was supported out by two nurses, who propped me in the corridor and gave me a glass of water.

'The world will never be same same again,' I said.

At this, they went off into gales of laughter. One threw her apron over her head to hide her mirth.

Not for twenty years did I visit John's home again. In the 1914–18 war he joined a Cavalry regiment, and later transferred to the Air Force which was so badly in need of recruits. In those days it was like flying in a matchbox tied up with string. He was killed in his aeroplane in 1918. I was by that time in Africa. I remember the mail arriving and my sister's letter telling me. It seemed like looking back on another life, those days at Lockwood Hall. But the distance in space and time could not eradicate the sadness of his death. I walked for days through my ordinary duties as in a dark dream from which I could not wake.

On my first furlough home I made an excuse to go and see his sister. I was to meet Alfred returning from America and Lockwood was not far away. Jane wrote back inviting me for a night. Both parents were dead; she had inherited everything. She put me to sleep in one wing, she slept with the dogs in the other, and a wide corridor seemingly a mile long separated us. I could not sleep. I wandered into the next room, of which mine was the dressing-room. The great four-poster was shrouded in dust sheets. I crept back and locked the door. I threw wide the window and looked out upon the summer's night. A lemon moon hung in the sky. Before me was a broad grass avenue with trees either side, throwing shadows over the grass. Below me were the double fan-shaped steps which led to the front door; a garden seat still stood there between the steps. We used to come out and sit there after lunch in the summer. To my right were the tennis courts where we had spent such happy hours and the old castle black against the sky. The owls were abroad hooting in melancholy. I turned away from the silence, heavy with memory, only to recall the shouts of laughter as we played hide-and-seek after tea, when the boys were dressed in our skirts so as to keep them from running too fast.

Next day Jane and I went to visit John's grave. We sat there quietly, overlooking the wide moor before us. We said nothing—only the curlew calling seemed an echo from the unknown of which he had been so unafraid.

8

BICYCLES THROUGH THE CONGO—1913

THE *Bicycling News* of the time would have been interested in the news-item of two Englishmen clearing their way through the Congo on bicycles, clad in knickerbockers to cover the knees from biting insects.

Father and Alfred had the time of their lives in more ways than one. Landing at Mombasa early in 1913, they were joined by three of Alfred's Cambridge friends. Fired by C.T.'s messages, they had joined the Mission in England and journeyed ahead. Owing to rumours which were rife about Father both at home and in Africa, that he was too old, his health poor and his head full of wildcat schemes, the meeting, to say the least, was not a warm one; and after much discussion the three broke away and joined another Mission. Father and Alfred were left to make their way alone. This was a great blow to both of them. But Father had trained his mind from early days to look upon every problem as an opportunity. In fact, I have known him to say that he welcomed 'tight corners', if only to see how God would get him out of them. Indeed, many a 'tight corner' was in store for them, as you will see.

Their route lay through Kenya and Uganda across Lake Albert, to the Belgian Congo—on and on through uncharted forests, among the teeming tribes whom nobody knew. But before they were even to reach Lake Albert, Alfred went down with a severe attack of fever. Then when his resistance was at its lowest, a cable arrived from his parents telling him to come back as he was evidently not old enough or strong enough for pioneering in the African forests. Father had great hopes for this journey. It was to lead them as pioneers of an army of recruits to the heart of Africa. Now it seemed as if he might lose his only companion. He would not persuade Alfred to carry on if he wanted to return, for while he was ready to face cannibals, wild animals and tropical diseases himself, it would be a different matter to be responsible for someone else's death.

Alfred lay all night thinking it out. He was still weak from fever, the tent was suffocating, the maddening zing of mosquitoes was like the top notes of a violin. Strange night sounds came from the forest so close around them—and beyond Lake Albert. Who knew what they might find? Dare he go on?

In the morning he had made up his mind. C.T. and he would face the future together whatever it might hold.

Three days' forest trek from Masindi brought them to the shores of Lake Albert. 'This morning, arrived at the foot of the hills on the east of the lake,' wrote Father. 'We looked across at the hills on the other side, the Belgian Congo, our promised land. Can you imagine our feelings?'

They crossed Lake Albert the next day and that night, their first in Congo territory, they camped on the lake shore. 'Dark came on,' his letter continues, 'and we had porridge for supper and a turn round in the bush to try for a buck, as we had precious little food. At dusk the mosquitoes and lake flies were a perfect pest. I slept in the open with the net, but had to shelter in the tent during the night because of rain. The flies provided a treble to the barking of the crocodiles—the lake was only twenty yards from our tent. I never knew crocs could make such a noise before and I took the precaution of keeping a good fire burning between my bed and the lake.'

He ended his letter with these words, 'I know I am God's. I know I only want His Glory and the salvation of others and I know He knows it. I never was better or stronger for years, but best of all, I know God is with us. He talks to me and His blessed Word means more than ever before and makes me burn to dare and do for Him.'

On their way next morning to make themselves known at the Belgian Post, Father said to Alfred; 'The next step is to get into the Belgian Congo. Can you speak French?'

'A bit of dog French that I learnt at school,' answered Alfred.

'Well, we ought to be able to manage,' said Father. 'They say the Belgians may not let us through their territory but when they've heard our French they'll probably let us do anything we want.'

Dog French it probably was, but the Belgians welcomed them and supplied the porters to take them on and guide them through the interminable forests ahead of them where it would be so easy to lose their way.

Their journey now lay through the fierce Balenda tribe who had killed Emin Pasha. The surrounding tribes stood in unholy terror of them and it was difficult to get porters. The few who came only ventured to do so because they would be travelling with white men. A short while before, a white man had come across from Uganda. He was taken to the Chief Julu who stripped his clothes off, beat him and sent him back naked. Recently, too, an English elephant hunter had been shot by a native of his tribe with a poisoned arrow in the shoulder and he had died before he could get help.

'You'll never come through alive,' a trader warned them before they left.

C.T.'s reply was, 'They'll be too interested in our bicycles to do anything to us.'

'Bicycles!' cried the trader, 'so you mean to say you are going to bicycle through the jungle?'

'Certainly,' said C.T. 'We'll get to the other end more quickly. And when they can't carry us we'll carry them.' He had an answer for everything and a faith big enough for any situation.[1]

They must have looked an odd procession with C.T. and Alfred in knickerbockers in the middle of the African bush, riding their cycles when they could, and carrying them over the roots and stumps in their path when they couldn't. In this region one day, cycling on ahead, C.T. suddenly called to Alfred, 'Can you hear the porters?' There was dead silence. They had lost their way. They cycled back, there was no sign of them. Then the tracks crossed and they took a wrong turn. On every side were massive trees, so tall that they turned the midday sunshine to twilight. Vegetation steamed with heat. A monkey or two swung from the lower branches gibbering at them. In the silence of the forest there were only the myriad sounds of tiny insects, birds and creaking branches. They felt as though a thousand eyes were staring through the thick bushes watching them. There was no doubt about it, they were lost in the primeval forest. The dwellers of the forest, if they were to meet them, would be their enemies, hunters with poisoned arrows, perhaps even cannibals. For three hours they went this way and that, they had no idea where they were going and the porters might now be twenty miles away.

Suddenly, they heard the snapping of twigs among the bushes. The next moment the trees parted and an almost naked African stood before them. In his hand he held a bow and some arrows. His teeth were filed down to sharp

1. With acknowledgements to *Well Played Sir*, by C. J. Davey, Eagle Book No. 61, Edinburgh House Press.

points, the unmistakable mark of the cannibal. For what seemed hours they stared at one another. Then C.T.'s gaze moved from the bow and arrows to the man's other hand. He carried a plaited basket and within it were some maize cobs and sweet potatoes. C.T. stepped forward, the cannibal stepped back. C.T. pointed to the basket and then to their very empty stomachs. The man set down the basket and C.T. went forward again and picked up some of the potatoes. Neither he nor Alfred had any money on them. Suddenly an idea struck Father, as he looked down at his cycling breeches.

'Why have knickerbockers got so many buttons?' he demanded of the bewildered Alfred. 'I'll tell you; to give to undressed cannibals.' In a moment he had ripped off half a dozen and given them to him. The man grinned and beckoned them to follow him. An hour or two later they were eating their dinner in the man's village. The food was well cooked by throwing it into the fire and pulling it out half an hour later, but they did not enquire what meat they were eating!

'A few more buttons settled the bill,' wrote Father. 'Their filed teeth declared our friends were indeed cannibals, but as both of us were lank, lean and tough, they were not tempted beyond what they were able; then we parted, Dei gratia, the best of friends and amidst considerable applause.' Eventually they were reunited with their porters and continued the journey.

At Kilo—a gold mining centre—they were to be detained for three months, partly because fresh porters were not forthcoming. They still lived in their tents and kept to their simple life, but the wet season was on in all its force and Father went down with the worst bout of fever he had ever had. An old snap shows the tents in the background and the cook squatting beside an open-air fireplace made up of three boulders. With one hand he holds over his head a piece of bent tin to keep off the rain, with the other he stirs some brew in a pot. There is no more depressing a picture and the whole scene is reflected in water—water everywhere. Father referred to his fever in his letters as like being repeatedly ducked by the devil.

'The biggest ducking was an ugly affair,' he wrote. 'The fever mounted, the weakness increased, all medicines failed. The darkest hour brought a brilliant flash of memory: "Is any sick, let him call for the elders of the Church, and let them anoint him with oil." Thank God for a saving sense of humour; there was but one elder and he was in his twentieth year. No matter. "One day is with the Lord as a thousand years." But where is the oil? Neither salad, olive or even linseed oil did we possess. "What's the matter with lamp oil?" "What, kerosene?" queried Alfred. "Why not? It is oil and that is all the Book says and we cannot afford to be narrow minded." The elder brought the lamp oil, dipped his finger, anointed my forehead and then knelt down and prayed. How God did it I don't know, nor do I care, but this I knew next morning, that whereas I was sick, nigh unto death, now I was healed.'

From Kilo to Arebi their track led through the Ituri Forest, where Stanley once travelled. The forest was very beautiful in places, like marching through an endless cathedral, the giant trees on either side representing columns. They could hear the African pheasants calling and the drip, drip, drip of the trees, but not a glimpse did they get of the forest denizens—the pygmies. The forest was so thick they could not shoot anything and so lived on bananas, bread and tea. This forest journey lasted eleven days.

From Arebi to Dungu the road improved and they were able to ride their cycles once again. At Dangu they met a real true friend, though hitherto they had been strangers, Count Ferdinand de Grunne, the Belgian District Commissioner. He not only looked after them, but gave them generous concessions at both Niangara and Nala, a country of luxurious grassland and forests and teeming with people—the biggest population in the whole of the Congo.

On arrival at Niangara, plumb in 'the very heart of Africa' as the explorer Dr. George Sweinfurth asserts it to be, they settled down for the time being. Having been confined for nine months in tents, they built a large mud and wattle house for £6 and called it Buckingham Palace.

From this home they trekked further south. They were not the first white men the people had seen. Traders and soldiers had gone before them. It was not many years since a Belgian officer with a troop of soldiers had set out to conquer some territory here. He had been warned that if he persisted he would probably be killed. He went on —and he and every soldier under his command died as they went through the cannibal country.

Yet these very folk listened to their preaching with joy and became Christians before many years had gone by. They taught them that Christ is God-made-man and died on the cross to save mankind; and that their faith should extend right through everyday life, guiding, instructing and comforting. They taught that being a Christian meant building first-rate houses, giving fair measure in the market place, living at peace with other tribes, making good homes and keeping the law and ruling for the people's good if you were a Chief.

9

AFRICA—THE MEETING—1917

THE step for me to the Mothers' Hospital must have been one in the right direction. From that time the plan to go to Africa became more possible. Father wrote that he was coming home to collect the first recruits. The Belgian Government had been generous in offering us sites for mission stations everywhere. But the men and women to man them were needed. Alfred was to stay in the Congo and look after the first Christian village that had sprung up—the village of Nala. As yet the Bangala lingua franca was not in print. He was to set himself to write it down.

Father arrived in England in 1916 and there followed nine months of travelling up and down the country. It was a busy time with Father speaking everywhere he was invited and interviewing would-be missionaries. Our home in Norwood, where Father had bought a house for £200, was the headquarters of the mission he was to bring into being. It was known then as the 'Heart of Africa Mission'. The house was always full of his friends who were to support him and candidates who had come forward at his meetings. At last he collected a nurse, a lady chemist and two Welshmen, and I was to be included.

The day for our departure came. I remember kissing Mother quickly, flying abruptly from the house for fear of crying and diving into the waiting growler. No more green a collection of would-be missionaries could you find anywhere. None of us was trained in any way for the hard and demanding life before us. So once on board my Father collected us each day and did his best to prepare us for what lay ahead. At times as I listened, a feeling of fear would creep over me. For four years I had been carried along by my engagement to Alfred and by circumstances that had evolved out of this. Now I was facing for the first time the hazardous adventure on which I had embarked. I questioned myself as I never had before.

Would I be going out to Africa if I had been single?

No.

Was I going out to Africa for Alfred?

Not entirely. I had announced my wish to be a missionary to the consternation of a friend when I was 18. Now I was 24.

Had I made all my decisions on the impulse of a moment, only to find myself drawing back, reluctant to proceed because of fear?

I surely was wanting. A reluctant missionary indeed!

Then there was the matter of my health. I had never been of the robust kind.

One night in my bunk, thinking it over, I said to myself in the dark 'I'll die, I know I'll die. I shan't be able to stick it.' Quick to follow my own thought came this—as though a word had been spoken to me by a person—'Thou shalt not die but live to tell of the wonderful works of God.' Next morning as Father sat writing in the opposite cabin I asked him where it came from.

'I think it is in one of the Psalms,' he said.

So some Sunday morning in church unbeknown to me I had no doubt sung this verse and it had been stored in my memory just to fit this occasion.

Father lectured us every morning on the saints of the Bible and their experiences and we were meant to follow their example. We sat round him looking naïvely hopeful, while our fellow passengers, mostly Belgian officials, eyed us with distaste. The unease the lectures produced was equalled by the war-time conditions under which we were travelling. All port-holes were blacked out. S.S. *Elizabethville*, following us a few weeks later, was torpedoed.

The sea journey took three weeks. On the last morning I was awake early and on deck to catch my first look at Africa. It was a brown line on the horizon of a dull grey sea. To those who are susceptible to her magic, Africa can cast a spell which binds you to her for ever. I still feel that magnetic pull whenever I set foot on her soil. The age-old earth at your feet, baked by an unremitting sun, sends a thrill through me to this day.

On arrival at Matadi at the mouth of the Congo River, striding about in a khaki Burberry suit, the jacket liberally supplied with pockets and a divided skirt for any emergency, I did my best to cope with this new world. For a few days we led a picnic existence at Matadi waiting for the twelve hour train journey to Kinshasa, which was later known as Leopoldville.

Here I was to have my first encounter with reality. It came almost as a blow between the eyes—me, the ass in the lion's skin—and she the first real woman missionary I was to meet on African soil. She was middle-aged, thin—thin as a sheet of paper. Everything about her was thin—her hands and face, her hair and clothes. My first conscious thought was, 'I hope I never become like this!' I had no idea in that short meeting that I was face to face with a dedication, a bravery and beauty of mind—for she was something of a poet—that I have perhaps never met since in a woman. She was then suffering from cancer which, being a nurse, she knew to be fatal unless treated immediately. Yet she never told her husband because it would hinder his work; and two years later when they reached the States it was too late and she died. There is a saying, 'The healing of the world is in its nameless saints.'

I was not ready for this truth which passed me by that day; I was busy here and there and she was gone.

Of the twelve hour train journey, I only remember the dreadful fact that every sleeper of that railway over which we slid with comparative ease had cost a life.

In Kinshasa we settled down to wait again for the Lever Brothers' boat to take us the first two hundred miles up the Congo River. Sunday morning dawned hot and stifling. We rummaged in our numerous boxes for something thin and tidy enough for Sunday. The men in pale khaki suits with clean handkerchiefs and we three women in our muslin and sola topis made our way on foot to a tiny chapel which I believe stands to this day. It was situated in a grove of dark mango trees; we thankfully sat down in the cool shade of the small House of God. The first hymn was announced, accompanied by a harmonium. It was a dirge-like tune, threatening us with death and its shadowy imminence. The verses were interminable and interspersed with each was a chorus which I shall never forget:

Death cometh once; hear now his tread,
Soon shall you and I be lying, each within
our narrow bed.

I was taken up with doing my best at singing, but when I sat down, I thought what a peculiar hymn it was to set before a party of newly-arrived missionaries. If I had had the least bit of humour ready that Sunday morning I would have laughed aloud, but in our serious frame of mind as we faced the unknown, I could only look at us all and wonder which one of us death would pick on first. I knew one thing definitely: it was not going to be me!

I seem to look back from a great distance on that eventful journey which in 1917 lasted four months. Once again I have the sense of the cool evenings on deck and see the Congo River miles wide, the gigantic virgin forests on either side, and I smell the sweet gentle fragrance of the frangipani wafted over the still water. In the day our cabins were stifling, though Father and I had been given the two front ones which caught what breeze there was. The day before I was to meet Alfred I had washed my hands in a basin in my cabin and throwing the water overboard my engagement ring flew off my hand and plopped into the mighty Congo River. Just a flash in the sun I saw it go by. That night, feeling that in some way this was an omen, I wrote in my diary these ponderous words. 'There are things in my past that I have to regret, but tomorrow begins a new day and I determine never to do an unkind or mean thing again.' I was soon to find that it takes more than determination to change character.

We were now on a much smaller steamer and the banks had become nearer. We stopped every night to refuel with wood from the forest. At last the morning dawned—the morning that I was to meet Alfred. I felt its full glory break upon me as I stole on deck. As I looked out there was no sign as yet of any station, so Father said in his most martial voice, 'All on deck for Bible reading.' My eyes continued to stray to the shore. We read through the interminable chapter of Acts 23 which deals with the trial of St. Paul before Ananias. It says something for my powers of concentration that I remember the chapter. My eyes were constantly searching the river bank as it twisted through the overhanging trees, which seemed to want to devour the river from either bank. At last we rose. A little clearing and a sandy beach apppeared. You could now see figures on the shore. More than four years had passed since I had seen Alfred. Inwardly I held my breath as if my whole being were for a moment suspended, so acute was the anticipation, the dread of what I might feel. My sister, Dorothy, had said when we parted, 'Promise me one thing. If, when you see him, you do not care, you will not marry.' And I had promised.

They touched my shoulder and said, 'There he is.'

'Where, where?'

'The one with the beard!' they said, laughing.

'No, no,' I said, 'it is not he! He would not meet me with a beard.' At last I caught sight of his figure on the shore. He had no beard!

It was upon the lower deck among the goats and chickens that we met. It was the same calm, unflappable Alfred, it was the same voice and the same man, but with a difference. He had a maturity that made him all the dearer to me. In that instant my apprehensions faded in recognition and love. I brought him up and showed him round. How proud I was of him, his battered topi and shabby coat with worn-out sleeves. Father had disappeared; presently he reappeared with a new coat upon his arm, and so we dressed Alfred up for the few days in touch with civilization.

There was much of the journey still ahead of us. Constant delays kept us waiting about as we changed into steamers of diminishing sizes. We wound our way slowly up the Congo and its tributary, the Welle River, for another week. Finally, the river journey was followed by a month's trek on foot. We had been travelling for four months in all when we reached our destination, Nala.

Nala, an old Belgian Fort, where we had started our work, was situated on the watershed of the Nile and the Congo. If you were to draw a line through the centre of Africa, from North to South and then again East to West, there would be Nala.

After all this travelling it is difficult to convey what it meant to enter a Christian village. For miles before we reached Nala, groups of Christians came out to meet us on the road and welcome us in. The people were naturally of a friendly disposition, but the greeting of the committee of twelve elders was warm with family feeling. Baragweni, the chief elder who had been a cannibal, had become a quiet, genial and wise person. I once asked him what human meat tasted like and he replied, 'Rich, mama, very rich indeed.'

Though we had been on the road since 6 a.m. it was high noon by the time we reached the centre of Nala. We found a clean, tidy, well-spaced village, avenues of palms grown years ago by the Belgians, interspersed with small and big houses, a church and a school house. They were built of mud and thatch in the simplest fashion. All this had been Alfred's work. And, into the bargain, he had completed the first stage of writing the Bangala vocabulary.

I well remember the feast spread out under the trees, with pineapples, bananas and tomatoes decorating the table. Four other missionaries had come in by the Nile and had arrived there before us, so that we must have sat down nearly a dozen to that first meal. We ate small roast chickens, mashed yams or manioc, fried sweet potatoes, native spinach of a rather strong flavour, followed by mangoes, pineapple, or bananas.

We found ourselves apportioned a new house each, a trained houseboy, a water carrier and a cook. There was no furniture at this stage; we simply spread out our camp equipment. Everything was organized. Alfred had completed the preparations down to the last detail and at last we were able to relax. He had instructed the elders and had started the school. He had trained servants for each new household. All this had been accomplished in the year he had been alone.

After three weeks' rest, which my Father badly needed,

we had to pack up again. This time it was to trek for a week to Niangara where the Belgian District Commissioner, the District Judge and various other Belgian officials were waiting to marry us. This was to be the first white wedding in the heart of Africa.

The other two in the party and myself were the only white women who had been allowed by the Belgians into the upper reaches of the Congo River. So far the Belgian officials were not permitted to have their wives with them because this part of the country was not considered civilized enough. Niangara was to become a flourishing centre of trade and is now a small town on the Uele River. Then it consisted of the few scattered brick houses of the District Commissioner, the District Judge, the doctor and the guest house.

Before we left England the Goslings of Hassobury had got into touch with Father because a brother had died at Niangara and they wanted a photo of his grave. This younger brother had come out to Congo to shoot an okapi. The species is a cross between a zebra and an antelope and had never been seen before by a white man. In fact its very existence was called in doubt.

Captain Gosling of the Rifle Brigade had shot his okapi and it was to be shipped back to England, but he had fallen ill with blackwater fever. He was brought back to Niangara. It was in this very house where he died that we were now gathered for the wedding. Passing in and out of the rooms I thought of him often. Father took Alfred and me that evening before the wedding to visit his grave and to take the promised photograph. I remember clearly how we stood round the grave and this thought came into my mind, 'But for God I should be in the grave and he standing here'. I quote from what I wrote at the time:

December 27, 1917. 'The journey is complete. We have

reached the heart of Africa. Upon a wide verandah I stand and watch the broad quiet Welle River sweep by. It is my wedding morning. There is no hurry anywhere. Every minute of it is ever in my memory. We had a service at our little mission station in the morning, the Africans crowded in. In the middle of the service an overloaded bench snapped in two and with muffled cries thirty of the congregation were shot on to the floor. How I caught Father's eye and nearly laughed. Then back to the Belgian post by canoe and lunch, followed by dressing for the official wedding. I do not forget that dressing. The day before I had worked to make the outfit complete. I was shocked to find that the shoes were white and the dress was cream. I put my hand to my head and bethought me of tea. I mixed the tea with the white powder and the shade was perfect and the shoes transformed and now I put on my dress. I was so busy I did not miss the sisters, but I needed them. I am so foolish and so young. I drape my hat with a veil, feeling it must have its place somewhere. The bridegroom, his trousers are a little short, his sleeves a trifle long and his too large shirt collar has a tuck put in at the back firmly held with a safety pin, but who cares. And when we sent the snapshots home, so sure of great applause—these sisters who are so frank and yet so necessary—they say, "You look like a bunch of trippers." '

The first wedding in the heart of Africa took but five minutes. The ten officials had all turned up in white. There was a great deal of bowing and 'Monsieur-ing' and signing of papers and all was over. Then tea and wedding cake to which the Belgian officials crowded in. Rukuruma, our first houseboy, was there, a very little Ruku. He handed round the cake with a solemn air.

We dined that evening with the Commissioner. He looked a little tired in the head from our bad French. So we made our departure at 9 o'clock and, saying goodbye to my Father, I stepped into a hammock and, with Alfred walking beside me, we made our way through the quiet night to the mission station about three miles away. I found again Alfred's work in the shape of a neat little house, with wide low windows looking out on the quiet waters of the river.

Next morning, to our consternation, we found a stray man of some neighbouring Mission had invited himself to breakfast. This made us pack up at once and go to a charming island up river where we spent many happy days. Here we pitched our camp and we called it 'Cherry-sand Isle' because of the long stretch of sand and because I wore a cherry-coloured coat.

Every day we made an expedition in the canoe and would come home at dusk. As we turned the bend in the river the island came in sight, with the little tents and fire and a tail of smoke mounting up to heaven. Of an evening, on the wide shore brilliant with warm moonlight, beside the silver river, we would walk and say nothing because, in our complete happiness, there was nothing to say. One night I woke with a start. There was a snorting and a puffing close at hand and looking to the river I saw a herd of hippopotami go by. Here upon the sand they had been used to sport but seeing others in possession moved on in disappointment.

10

A HOUSE OF MUD

DURING those first years in Africa, I was amazed how comfortable mud houses could be made. With a couple of coats of whitewash inside and a thatched roof, they had a cosy cottage look. They could be designed in any shape to suit your liking. We had a living-room, open verandah, bedroom and a bathroom next door. The waterman filled up the huge clay debbies every morning with water. The camp bath stood in a recess, where with a hole in the wall any overflow of water ran away outside. There were many ingenious ways of putting up curtains where necessary and making bamboo towel rails.

Our food was entirely that of the country, except for an occasional cup of tea on Sundays and perhaps a soda loaf. Father always said that as long as we missionaries travelled first class, lived out of tins, ate bread and butter and drank tea, the world would never be evangelized.

I shall never forget the first breakfast in our own home at Nala. Alfred had spoiled me on our honeymoon, letting me down lightly, allowing me to open tins freely. When I came to sit down to that first breakfast, there was boiled rice, chicken that tasted like string, boiled yams like mashed potatoes, no butter, no bread, no tea, no milk, just a glass of cold water. I was a little surprised to find how much I minded. I soon set to and found ways of doing this and that, so that in a year or so I had twenty-six ways of cooking chicken.

We learnt from the Africans how to make oil from flying ants by using the ingenious African method. During the flying ant season fires were made at night, the ants flew to the fires and their wings were singed off. They were collected in flat baskets and dried in the sun. So fat were they that they seemed to be made of liquid oil in a tiny cellophane capsule. When completely dry they rustled together as you moved them. They were then boiled in water for some time and the oil, rising to the top, was skimmed off. This made a very good frying substitute in cooking, being tasteless. The native palm oil which the Africans used for their food was a thick tomato-coloured grease and had a strong flavour.

We also made sugar from sugar cane. The women brought the bundles of cane in on Saturday. They stripped off the bark on Monday and pounded it with much chanting until the pith was broken. Then it was put into home-make squeezers made of bark twine and two men wrung it like washing until the juice poured out. The juice was then put into big cauldrons and set on three stones and boiled for one and a half days. At first we found the sugar was acid and then someone looked up in an encyclopaedia to see how sugar was made and found potash was the answer. So at the end of the boiling a spoonful of ash from beneath the cauldron was put in. It frothed and became sweet, some of it as soft and pale as sand.

Among many vegetables there was very good spinach, tomatoes and many fruits. We were not badly off once we got round to knowing how to use the indigenous foods.

On market day, Saturdays, tomatoes, English potatoes, eggs, pineapples, mangoes, bananas, monkey nuts (another source of oil or butter) all poured in to Nala. There would be a service at one side of the market to which some 500 people would come, representing as many as twelve different tribes. I never knew of any fighting, though skirmishes did take place sometimes outside the Christian village. Markets were made an occasion, and anyone who had the good fortune to own a piece of cloth wore it, no matter how small; pieces from the size of a pocket-handkerchief to a table-cloth were equally fashionable. Otherwise a bark fan-shaped affair was worn by the women and a G-string for the men. The Avongara were the royal clan of the Azande tribe. They had proud, classic features. The women's hair-do's were of a beauty beyond description: great high diadems, branching outwards made by weaving the hair on a basketwork frame. With their bodies oiled, you would find on a market day every lovely shade of brown from deep mahogany to pale chocolate.

For some months we had only our camp equipment; then we took to making packing cases into furniture. It was not long before we were able to get some two-handled saws. The word went round and sawyers, carpenters, basket-makers and anyone who could wield a hammer came to live amongst us. They sawed down trees and made planks. Chairs, tables, beds and shelves for books soon appeared. Father, however, lived to the end of his days with his simple camp furniture. Alfred would have done the same but I persuaded him out of it. I did not see the point of wearing out an expensive camp bed when there was a perfectly good wooden one to sleep on. However, we were always warned not to get so posh that it would make more barriers between us and the Africans.

Father was quite blatantly unconventional. The Church at home he thought had become more a building than a way of life. He especially objected to the wearing of 'women's apparel' as he put it and intoning the service. 'What son would speak to his father in such a voice?' As to the variety of sects, he declared he belonged to them all. But when announcing the hymn 'Onward Christian

Soldiers' at a meeting I have heard him stop at verse 4 and say 'We will omit this verse because it is not true.'

All one body we,
One in hope and doctrine,
One in charity.

He had not been ordained. He read in his Bible, which was his constant guide as to how the early Christians went about things and he would do the same. So that he baptized, dedicated, married and gave Communion and buried them in his simple African village church, as though his had been the mighty ordination of God Himself. Morning prayers were at 7 a.m. when the whole village would turn up. Work began at 7.30 or so. Father led all meetings with his banjo which he had learnt to play while at Eton. I am told Africans understand banjo music better than a harmonium—certainly the singing lost nothing in the swing. They would raise the roof with the hymns of Moody and Sankey translated into Bangala. Sometimes there would be a testimony meeting. Once a man got up and told us a story of such relish that every head turned in his direction.

I was so interested that I whispered to Alfred, 'What is he saying?'

Alfred replied, 'He has just told us he is sorry he has to confess that he has eaten his uncle.'

The Prayer Meeting every Friday night in the huge open-sided palaver house was a thing to remember. Outside in the dark the palm trees rustled gently in the evening breeze. Inside one could see some 200 bowed figures, their oiled bodies shining in the light of the palm oil lamps. Gemisi, the converted cannibal and ex-soldier, was the churchwarden. He would take upon himself the duty of prowling around and if by chance he caught anyone with their eyes open he gave their heads a good duck and told them that was no way to behave in God's house. When a man went on praying too long, carried away by the new wonderful experience of speaking to God, my Father would say, 'Now, we'll sing a hymn while our brother finishes.'

They say you cannot change human nature or that such changes take generations. I can only say I saw it happen in very much less time and I know over the years that with many—though not all—the change has lasted. One man in his youth had been in the Belgian Army in charge of prisoners. Stories were told of his brutality: he would take a dislike to a prisoner and while on work would pick a quarrel with him and shoot him on the spot. He would then go back and tell his Belgian sergeant the man tried to run away. This man was so alarming to look at that as I went to school one afternoon and saw him coming, rather than meet him I took a short cut among the bushes. On market day he would bring a plate of tomatoes for me to buy. The house would be empty, everyone having gone to the market. He would sit on the verandah and cough to make his presence known to me. Being a no-good missionary, I would hide behind my bedroom door and peep at him through the crack instead of coming out and talking about God, as Father or Alfred would have done. But I saw this man change. Everything about him changed: his face, his voice, his manner. As he learnt about and accepted the Grace of God he surely became a new man. The last person we visited in his village outside Nala before we came away on furlough was this man. He sat before his hut with his leg up on a stool, for he had an ulcer. He said, 'I have walked many a mile through the forests on these legs to do my own will. Now I have given myself to God, I only wait for my wound to heal and I shall use them to preach the Gospel.'

It was during our second year in the Congo that we started boys' and girls' boarding schools in Nala. The two schools were at opposite ends of the village and there must have been about fifty students in each. When the boys were locked up in their dormitory at night, by the light of a fire in the centre of the room, they would take off the missionaries: 'This is how Bwana Davy walks. And this is how Mama Bakisi (Buxton) talks in the kitchen,' was overheard one night, followed by screams of laughter.

Father was often having bouts of fever at this time, which he found increasingly difficult to throw off. Alfred had been getting up at midnight to visit him and give him a cup of tea. On just such a night Alfred was sleeping so deeply I had not the heart to wake him. But the thought of Father kept nagging at me. Finally I got up and lit the hurricane lantern. As I put the match to the wick, it passed through my mind that only recently a leopard had seized a small boy returning to his village nearby one evening and carried him off like a chicken into the jungle and he was never heard of again. And a woman had been pounced upon and taken off early one morning as she was scooping up water from the stream, within a few yards of her hut. All that was left was her earthenware bowl half full of water and the cup lying in the stream. Then I comforted myself that the watchmen would be in a hut at the further side of the parade ground. All the same I hurriedly put on my dressing-gown, in case I should turn back, and went out into the night.

What a wonderful sight met my eyes! Nala was drenched in moonlight. High overhead the moon hung like an alabaster lantern in a shining silver dome. It was inky black under the palms and there was a lacework of light and shadow at my feet. Not a breath of air stirred the warm still night.

I scurried across the garden passing a banana tree with its great sweeping leaves spread outwards. I saw a drop of dew like a diamond set in the middle of the curve of the leaf. It ran down the stem as I brushed past and extinguished itself on the ground. I walked more slowly across the parade ground, because I could see further. The night watchmen leapt up as I came near to their hut and sttod at attention beside their seven-foot spears like Roman soldiers. I told them my errand and went on into the garden surrounding Father's house.

As I climbed the steps to the verandah he woke. The crisis was over, he was having his first refreshing sleep. It was a pity I had come. All the same I was not going back without giving him that cup of tea. I called the house-boy who was sleeping in the outhouse and soon a fire was burning on the back verandah and the kettle making its cosy sounds. As we sat over our tea I regarded Father secretly. He lay back on his camp bed. It seemed I looked at him over a great gulf, fixed. His face was drawn and yellow, his eyes hollow in his face. There was little sign left of the strong cricketer. It was not pity I felt, but a wonder. Here was my Father, a man I had never really known; he had given up everything for a purpose, to bring the Gospel to the Africans. He had taken the high way. I had never done so. I was in Africa because of Alfred. I was on the low road. It was not possible for us ever to meet.

He broke in on my thoughts. 'You are not my only night visitor,' he said. 'Two nights ago Kamu arrived on the verandah.' He was one of our weaker brethren. The houseboys had long since gone to bed. Standing there in the dark with a lighted piece of wood in his hand, for protection as well as light, he had given Father quite a start.

'I could not sleep, Bwana,' he said. 'Lying on my bed in my hut I was thinking of you here ill—and no one to pray for you, so I have come to do just that.'

Kamu thereupon knelt down and in the manner of any visiting parson, put his elbows on the camp bed, put his hands together and proceeded to pray. His prayer was almost an argument with the Almighty. 'Here is your child, Bwana, sick and you have not healed him. Alone in the night, as you see, I have come to pray to you for him.' After this he proceeded to bring to God's notice the wide world, as he knew it, referring to 'our brothers here and our brothers there.' By the time he was half way round the full-scale trip, Father was asleep. When he woke at 3 a.m. his black brother had gone. Coincidence or not, Father was better for the visit.

We smiled as we talked on. Then I plumped up Father's pillows. But as I turned the last one, there was a pistol underneath.

'Why a pistol?' I asked, for we never carried fire-arms.

'Well,' said Father, rather apologetically, 'a few nights ago a leopard paid me a visit. He stood there at the foot of the steps with his two front paws on the first step and looked curiously up at the verandah.' (Father slept without a mosquito net and in the open kati-kati[1] to get more air. He would cover himself with verbena essence against mosquitoes and hope for the best.) 'So I thought I'd be ready for him,' he added.

'Leopards again,' I thought and hurriedly prepared to leave.

My journey back was uneventful, but on reaching our house I took one bound on to the verandah, dived into the doorway and shut it firmly, leaning against it. 'Thank God for doors,' I said to myself, for I had once had to sleep without a door in a leopard-infested village. I

1. Large open verandah linking two rooms.

looked around—the blessed familiarity of things! There stood my dressing-table with brush and comb on it; there the bedside table with Bible and candlestick. I placed the lantern on the floor to keep the light down. Alfred had not stirred, I crept into bed and with a deep sigh of relief, I slept through the dawn to a new day.

It was towards the end of my second year in Africa that my daughter, Susan, was born. The Salvation Army Hospital had stood me in good stead. I was not afraid. I had had various parcels from my Mother, with every imaginable thing—even instructions for dealing with a cleft palate! A newly published book from America, by a New Zealander, Truby King, filled me with panic on account of what I had *not* got and so eventually I put it away. One thing I did glean from it was that I must eat as much fruit as possible. Here the ubiquitous banana played a part. I think I had them at every meal.

A missionary trained in midwifery was to be with me for a month, but she warned Father that should anything go wrong there was little she could do by herself. Father took an original precaution. He had an arrangement with the drummer of each village between Nala and Niangara where the only doctor was. The huge drums could relay messages over miles of forest. A message was worked out which would reach Niangara in less than half an hour. 70 per cent of most of the African languages have a tonal quality and can therefore be transmitted on the drum. The different notes of the drum are synonymous with musical notes. The sound of the drum reproduces the sound and rhythm of the human voice in each individual native language. Niangara was six days journey away, so that the doctor could only have arrived after any need for him had long passed. But this bush telegraph gave some reassurance to Father and Alfred.

It was Saturday, with the market in full swing, when Susan entered this life, after only two hours of discomfort. I won the race with two others, African women, who were twelve and sixteen hours in labour. Bananas or no, she appeared with banana-coloured hair and when I asked to see her it was she who gave me the most intelligent stare, as much as to say, 'What sort of a mother am I landed with?'

At the end of the month Miss Chapman left me alone with the boxes and outfits, the Truby King book and this newcomer. At first I was scared stiff. Then another mother came to Nala and told me in a matter-of-fact voice that babies did not die as easily as all that.

As time went by I gained confidence. The Christians came by ones and twos and gave her charming gifts, a potato patch, a bunch of bananas (her signature tune) and even a one cent piece. At three months we were such experienced parents that Alfred decided to go out on trek to preach in the villages with us in tow. In those days I did not question anything, so along Susan and I went. But Father, living now at Ibambi, sent a runner post-haste after us to ask, 'Are you mad?'

I was glad to get back to my quiet home, for everywhere the Africans had thronged to see her, gazing pop-eyed on the first white baby they had seen. On one occasion she had burst into tears in such a grown-up fashion that I was sure it was doing her no good. She was a very aware child, even at that early age. On one of our journeys by canoe, she shrieked like a sixteen-year-old every time we shot the rapids and whirled into the cascading torrents.

11

THE VILLAGE OF PALMS

NALA was a quiet place hidden away among a myriad feathery palms. The days and years dreamed themselves away under this cool canopy of shade. There were days of slow, happy routine in this island of life. There were leisurely evenings when we went calling in the African village which had grown up around us. Each road that fanned out from the compound was lined with palms rattling their long leaves overhead in the evening breeze as we walked. And in the morning the lane to the stream would be crowded with watermen and village women going down to fetch water. At the back of each house, washing would appear to dry in the sun, while by the afternoon the kitchen boys of each household made their way with arms piled high with saucepans to wash them in the sandy river bed below. Now and then the mail runner would arrive in red fez first seen through a tunnel of palm trees, waving their flags as if to greet the arrival of so important a person.

I was standing on the verandah of our house one morning, admiring the scene before me. Mother had sent me a box of seeds and the gardener had planted them in two beds on either side of the walk. To shelter them I had had a fence of twigs put round the freshly turned earth. To my left ran the wide avenue, a beautiful shady walk of palms grown thirty feet high. Looking up as you strolled here, it was like a vast cathedral that had slept for a hundred years. This avenue led south out of Nala to

Ibambi. As I stood there I saw out of the corner of my eye an African and his wife, followed by a porter carrying his tin box, coming along the avenue. The man was dressed in European clothes of various assortments and with a particularly large pair of boots on his feet. At sight of me he charged across the budding garden; he ploughed through the twig fence into the flower beds, boots and all, followed by his wife with her big flat feet and the porter.

'Hi,' I shouted, in a most unmissionary tone of voice, 'mind those flower beds. Don't go that way, come this way.'

He did not seem to hear me. They came on full tilt. By this time I was quite annoyed and was asking him what he meant by this onset, when Alfred came from his room. Calm, quiet, with a welcoming smile for all at any time of day or night, he held out his hand to the man. No one took any notice of me.

Gamutu, for that was his name, was a big strong Azande. He took Alfred's hand in both of his.

'Bwana,' he said, 'I have walked two hundred miles to come and hear about God. I was in my village when a man came through and told us that at Nala you taught about God. I have always wanted to know about God. So my wife and I packed up at once and here we are.'

After some talk Alfred found him a house in the workmen's village on the compound and saw to it that he had some food.

As Alfred left them, Gamutu said, 'When is the first lesson?'

From that time he never missed a meeting, whether the early morning one with the workmen, or the Friday night prayer meeting, or the Sunday services. He was always there, sitting quietly with an intent look on his face. Soon he was taking part in the prayer meetings, in which all the Christian community would join. I did not understand a word he said, for he would pray in his own tribal language, but I always listened arrested when he prayed. While others prayed round the whole wide world, giving you time to count backwards from a hundred, his prayers were short and eager words to the God he had longed to know. It seemed that a hush came over us and I felt the presence of God among us in the quiet night.

Gamutu began his work as an ordinary workman. He soon rose through the rank and file, becoming a gang leader. He took responsibility well; then one day he became chief of the workmen. Finally, he was given the trusted position of head of the Boys' School, while Gamisi was away on trek.

The months went by, Gamutu trying his hand at reading and writing. He had been with us nearly a year when one evening an urgent message came from Miss Dennis. She was a nurse and had been overseeing the building of a new hospital.

'Come down to the new hospital,' she said. 'I have Gamutu ill with pneumonia.'

The building loomed up as we came with hurricane lantern across the playground, a long mud hut with thatched roof. It was furnished in utmost simplicity with bamboo beds and a red rug on each. We found Ma Deni sitting beside Gamutu, who was the only patient. The paraffin lamp threw a beam of light over the dark mud walls on to the two figures. Alfred went down on one knee beside him and Gamutu put his hot hand in his.

He spoke urgently, as he always had, as though there was little time. 'Bwana,' he said, 'I know I am dying but I am going to be with God.'

Alfred assured him that he would get better, the medicine would do its work. Then he prayed for him. But Gamutu looked at him and said, 'Do not grieve. I know this is the end and I know where I am going. I go to God.'

He lasted through the night but at dawn, with Ma Deni and Alfred beside him, he went to be with the God he had sought so urgently and found with such assurance.

They buried him that afternoon. My baby, Susan, had been restless and I was pacing the verandah with her in my arms when the little funeral procession passed down the palm avenue beside my house, the very path he had come down to enter Nala so short a time ago. I thought with regret of my harsh greeting. A light rain was falling and the sun was trying to shine. They passed by, but not with the wailing that accompanies pagan funerals, but singing an old negro spiritual. The sound rose and fell on the soft air. It ran like this:

Away over Jordan
With my blessed Jesus,
Away over Jordan
There'll be no partings there.

The Christian community would have had it explained to them that Jordan was a river depicting the line between life and death. But as I turned the corner of the verandah, rocking Susan to and fro, I did wonder if the pagans were turning over in their minds, 'We know the name Jesus, but who is this Jordan?'

I could not forget Gamutu. We missed him. Nala seemed to have lost someone who had been good for us all. Especially I missed him on Friday evening at the prayer meeting. A year later we were to return home on furlough. One of the last things I did was to find his grave. The jungle had grown over it. I had to battle with the undergrowth this way and that, then suddenly I came upon the mound. On top, his enamel plate was turned upside down and a rusty tin spoon lay beside it. I did not really know why I had come. I stood there looking down on the grave. All about me was silence, except for a few birds twittering in the palms overhead. Was it because from the beginning I had been unconsciously watching him—a man who in one short year had come from the twilight of pagan faith into the light of God? And was this my humble tribute to him who had brought me on many a Friday evening into the presence of God?

Dreams are important to Africans. Here are two examples:

1. One day a man from the bush arrived at Ibambi at express speed from an outlying village, to tell this tale. This is how he related it. A man who had been at one of the Ibambi market meetings and heard the Gospel, had died. All the tests had been made on him to be sure he was dead, such as applying a burning stick to the soles of his feet. He was quite dead and, after 24 hours, his body had been wrapped in bark cloth and put on a bamboo bed to be taken to his grave. Four men were in the act of carrying him, the mourners behind weeping loudly in chant, when suddenly he had sat up on the bier. The bearers lost no time in putting him down, almost dropping him in their fright, and with cries of terror everyone scattered in every direction, leaving the once dead man to make his way out of the cocoon of bark cloth in which he had been wrapped. He walked back to his hut and by degrees the frightened villagers gathered round him.

He told this story: 'I have been with God. I saw Him and He saw me. He knew my name and that I had heard the Gospel at Ibambi. God said to me, "Why have you not listened to my message?" I felt ashamed and had no answer. After a while God said, "I will give you one more chance. You shall go back to your village for ten days. Send for the preacher, accept the message, and then you shall come back to me." '

A native Christian from Ibambi at once accompanied the returning messenger and for ten days he told the Gospel to the people. The old man was apparently quite well during this time and became a Christian; but on the tenth day he said to his friends, 'Now I am going back to God.' Then he very simply lay down and died. They packed him up once more for eternity, rolling him up in his bark cloth and pinning it either end with 5 inch-long thorns from the forest, and this time he did not sit up on the bier.

2. Jabori was a sub-chief of the Azande tribe living near Nala. A kind, good man with white hair, he came to every service from the time Nala was opened as a Mission Station. One day he told Alfred that one night many years before we missionaries arrived, God met him in his sleep and said, 'White people will come. They will come with a message from me. Listen carefully and do what they tell you. Until then do only what is right.'

He said that since then he had done his best to carry out the instructions and, indeed, he had the reputation of being an exceptionally upright old man.

I said to Alfred, 'Do you think he became a Christian from the time God spoke to him?'

He said, 'Yes, I think so.'

'Well,' I said, 'that means he received the grace of God without knowing anything about Christ.'

And Alfred said, 'Yes—Come to think of it, Abraham in the Bible was a man of God knowing nothing of Christ.'

Every well-regulated household consisted of a cook, a house-boy and a waterman. The latter's duty was to keep the house and kitchen supplied with water from the stream. From my bedroom window I could see the small path down to the river lined with mango trees, shady and cool. Here all the watermen of Nala meet and greet and jibe each other and trot on, pail on head and green leaf steadying the water.

Miyeye, or Mr. Egg, was my water carrier. He was not prepossessing; he was young, yet he had a little old face, a high-pitched voice and as I interviewed him on the day of his entering my service, I noticed he had no ears. It looked as if they had been nipped off by a rat in the night. 'Miyeye, where are your ears?' I wanted to say. But I controlled myself and the question was not asked. He came and went in and out of our house. I never saw him but the question burned on my lips, 'Miyeye, where are your ears?' but something restrained me.

It was a Monday night. I know it was Monday, because we always made sugar on Monday from the cane bought off women at Saturday's market. Under a bright starry sky Miyeye sat stirring the last pot of sugar. All day he had tended three fires in a row each with a sugar pot boiling in the sun. I came out and sat beside him. Zeleda, the houseboy, squatted the other side of the fire. The fires made us conversational. The moment had come. The poignant question, so long held in check, popped out, 'Miyeye, where are your ears?'

He stood, lighted a wisp of straw, gazed into the sugar pot to see that all was well and quietly sitting back on his haunches replied, 'Madam, I have eaten them.'

'Eaten them!' I exclaimed in astonishment.

'Yes, eaten them,' said Miyeye calmly. 'Long years ago I was a slave in a chief's village. My life was hard. I did much work and was never paid. One day I talked with one of the chief's wives and together we decided to run away. The night came and we ran and ran and ran. But the chief missed us and sent his soldiers after us. I was but a boy and she a woman and we had not gone far. In a big ring, our fate was decided. A big pot was put on to boil and I saw the woman laid on the ground and dismembered limb by limb, and limb by limb put into the pot to boil before her own still conscious eyes. Slowly she was quartered and boiled up to be eaten and it was my turn next. Suddenly into the circle there comes the chief's head wife. Gesticulating wildly, she says, "Oh, chief, it is not good to eat a child, a curse will come upon us. We shall die." My fate was turned and instead the chief gives judgment that I am to eat my own ears.' Miyeye went on, 'Ah, mama, it was terrible and I was very, very ill for days.'

For some time we sat silent. I shivered and looked behind me into the black shadows. The night sounds wove a web around us, the flip of leaves in the night breeze and the boiling of the sugar.

Sunday morning in Nala! After a busy market day you could feel the quiet creeping on you on Saturday night as the notes of the Last Post died away and all was silence. Then out of the long night came Sunday fresh and new. For one thing we all wore different clothes. Small Bako, one of the school children who worked for me in the house, was the one who of all our boys somehow gave the grandest air to Sunday. His shirt was spotless, his little tight pants were faultless. One such Sunday he handed me buttered egg at breakfast and left behind him an exquisite aroma. It seemed familiar. Raising my eyebrows I said as quietly as possible, 'Bako, you have been using my lavender water.' He laid aside the buttered egg and fetched and placed within my hands his purchase at yesterday's market—a cheap little bottle of scent. I was abashed. But his toilet was not finished here. Lying like glittering gold upon his nut-brown neck was powder, as if made of sandalwood. He saw my eye again upon him and he pointed and said, 'It is foolish, but it is for show.' I smiled, I knew just how he felt.

The first real sound in the Mission clearing was about 10.45, on a Sunday morning, when away in the distance you heard a mêlée of beating drums and bugles. It was the boys' school mustering for parade. Never did I hear the advancing band and measured tread but I ran to the verandah to watch them pass. Sixty little boys, all oiled and combed and clad in white cotton loin cloths. The first two swung a rattle each from side to side. The next two had the same. Then followed four little buglers, two by two, eyes aflame, cheeks bursting. Following them, two little drummers and another two behind. The boys' school: each had his own special way of marching. There was such an enormous swagger about this five foot nothing band of Nala that I would slip behind the pillar and laugh, and yet it was at once a pathetic and stirring sight. Once a visiting American, seeing them advancing down the palm avenue of Nala on such a Sunday morning, had also hidden behind a pillar, but it was to hide tears of compassion. There was Gima, a little ill-fed thing, and there was big strong Aiba, the smart-Alec of the school who on one occasion had to receive paternal correction and had padded his clothes with newspaper. At the rear was Gemisi, the ex-Belgian soldier, now captain of this small, motley throng. He wore a red tunic, brass buttons and all; breeches which were once white, boots several sizes too large and a red fez to crown a face as shiny as polished ebony.

The rest of us gathered slowly. Bako took my chair on his head and placed it in church. The women would struggle with the temptation to come in late and create a sensation. Inevitably they would arrive late, and we were already singing our first hymn.

The singers meant well, but there was one note which did not suit African throats so they would substitute another. The boys' school sang till their veins stood out and, when we settled down to listen, some leant against their brothers in exhaustion. Mbikasi, the baby of the boys' school, fell asleep. He had nothing to lean against and swayed to and fro. I thought of his mother away in the bush and crept forward and led him to my chair. Of the Avongara Tribe, he had a skin like golden satin, a tiny basket-work hair-do rose above his neat little face. And the eyes—they were the eyes of a baby gazelle, to melt any heart. He sat on my knee with his little brown head against my shoulder and slept content through the sermon. When we rose to sing the last hymn and I set him down, I was palm oil from head to foot!

In Africa the unexpected often happens and I have watched aghast one dog chase another round the pulpit until the preacher looked quite dizzy. I heard many sermons with Flossie, the white terrier, snoozing under the pulpit. One day Nikuti, who had no sense of time, gave us an illustration of climbing the flagstaff: 'And when the man has reached half way up, tired, he rests for half an hour.' The picture of the unfortunate chap clinging to the flagstaff for half an hour was altogether too much for some of us.

Then would come the closing hymn and collection. A grass hat was put on the table and each brought his offering to the front—money, eggs, buttons would be placed in the hat. Each one would hesitate and look around to see who would be first, until at last one brave one stepped out and soon the stream followed.

We congregated outside and exchanged greetings. I shook hands with one, Mbongo, which being interpreted means elephant. I said laughing, 'Oh, Mbongo, you slept in the sermon; with these two eyes I saw you, and more, it was the sleep of deceit, for you slept with your head up as though you were listening.'

'Ah, mama, never again, I will never do it again.'

It was on a Sunday evening as we sat with my Father and about six missionaries, having one of those rare cups of tea, that the two nightwatchmen appeared on the verandah with their spears gleaming in the dark. Nancy, from the girls' school, had been caught by Chief Abiangama on her way back to school.

'He has kept her prisoner,' they explained urgently. 'We have already been to the village to demand her back, but he will not let her go.'

Nothing appealed to my Father more than an adventure of this kind. He immediately ordered the alarm to be blown on the bugle in the centre of the parade ground. It was not long before all the Christians of the village poured out of the palm groves, having picked up on the way anything they could lay their hands on. Sticks, wood out of the fire, pangas,[1] rakes and hoes were among the variety of weapons in the company. They congregated, some fifty of them, at the foot of the steps leading to Father's house. Father, from the top of the steps, addressed the eager throng. He was no pacifist, but on this occasion he ordered everyone to lay down their weapons and go to the rescue of Nancy as Christians and not as soldiers. There was a murmur of disappointment in the crowd, but one by one they laid down their arms in a pile at the foot of the steps. Father had been suffering from fever, so Alfred saw to it that his hammock was brought out and, in the hands of four strong men, Father was born aloft at the head of the procession. We women missionaries were each put in charge of a Christian elder.

1. Long knives used for cultivating.

It must have been quite an hour's trek through the forest before we came to the Chief's village. But long before our arrival we had heard the drums beating and the guttural cries of the dancers. As we approached we saw a circle of about two hundred men dancing, oiled bodies gleaming and a bunch of feathers on every head. They swayed in time to the drums. Father ordered his men to break through the circle and we all poured in after him. They stopped opposite the Chief and Father got down from his hammock. Seizing Abiangama by the beard he demanded the return of Nancy. The Chief backed away saying, 'I'll fetch her, I'll fetch her!'

But Father, not to be taken in, followed in pursuit. There began the most ridiculous chase among the huts of his numerous wives, the Chief dodging and Father cutting him off, with the whole band of Christians following on the trail. Suddenly there was a cry of 'Bunduki!' (guns!) on all sides, and although the guns probably would not go off, this was too much for the unarmed Christians, who fell upon the tribesmen with their bare fists. There never was heard such a thumping and pounding and, in the darkness, all you could see were the bobbing feathers of the warriors and the flying shirt-tails of the Christians as they laid into each other. This must have gone on for five minutes when I found my way to Father, who was looking a bit nonplussed. It was going to be difficult to get us out of this, for our fifty men and women were ill-matched to take on two hundred warriors. At this crucial moment, when the confusion was at its height, I remembered the orderly singing procession that had set out from Nala with such good intentions. I started to sing in a piping voice, a familiar Christian hymn. It was the first hymn I was taught as a child and the first hymn to be translated into the Bangala language:

Jesus loves me! this I know,
For the Bible tells me so;
Little ones to him belong,
They are weak, but he is strong.

Voices joined in and it became quite a chorus; strange as it may seem, slowly, one by one they ceased to fight.

As the battle died down one of the Chief's wives made her way on all fours through the mêlée of legs until she reached Father, when she quickly took his little finger in her teeth and bit it as only a cannibal can. Father let out a yell and I looked down to see what was happening. Seeing the Chief's wife was the source of the trouble, and forgetting Father's message to us of no violence, I gave her a thump which sent her sprawling in the dust.

There was a lull in the turmoil and Father now saw that there was an opportunity to call a halt. Drawing a line on the ground, he shouted to all Christians to come on one side, and the pagans on the other. Looking rather more dishevelled than when we arrived, the Christians gathered together and formed up into procession once again, marching off to the tune of another hymn.

Meanwhile Nancy, who had been padlocked in a hut, took advantage of the noise outside to work her way through the reed walls. She escaped, and, running back to Nala, arrived there ahead of her rescuers.

12

THE TESTING

MANY people have sought to describe their experience of turning towards God. For some it has been in an instant, on a resolve of the will. To others it has been through absorbing day by day the teaching and example of those around them. Whether the experience is called a change of heart, or conversion, or by any other name, whether it is instantaneous, or slow, the reality of meeting with God is the common factor between them all. Any of these adventures produce change of direction; but learning to keep that direction, through the frustrations and obstacles of life, takes nothing short of a lifetime.

Before I went out to Africa, I had had to speak at various farewell meetings, as is the custom with missionary societies. I had actually thrown my weight about quite a bit and said something of all the great things I was going to do as a missionary, giving the impression of how dedicated I was. Now and again a note of honesty would creep in; in one such moment of truth I said, 'I am really going to Africa because where the carrot is there the donkey goes,'—and as Alfred had red hair this was received with applause.

Long before we reached Nala I knew I did not fit. I did not like my fellow missionaries and I am quite sure they did not like me. I became critical, often speaking ill of my neighbours. I was bored. Had I not been happily married, I could not have stood the isolation. There is no place like Africa for finding you out.

One of my jobs was to teach reading and writing to a class of small boys. Furnished with a whistle and a switch, not to beat the students but to smack the desk in the hope of keeping order, I would sally forth of an afternoon to do my stuff. There is no denying they were attractive, with their big eyes, squat noses and woolly heads. Clean and prim in their white clothes, there was something of the gentlemen of learning about them, anyway to begin with. As I got bored, so they got out of hand and much smacking of the desk and whistle blowing was necessary. 'Oh, to get home,' I would think, letting my eyes wander to the palm trees waving outside, 'It is Thursday, the runner will be in from Rungu, letters from home and a cup of tea!' And with one last blast of the whistle I would shout, 'Kazi kwisha!' which meant, 'Work finished.' adding in my mind, 'thank goodness!' They would dive in a mass for the door and I, with some semblance of dignity, would wend my way home in the shade, to the letters and the tea.

Yes, that shouting! I was inclined to shout. The children were possible, the elders were endearing, but the ordinary run of native did not interest me. Indeed, sometimes I wondered why I had got there at all. We had a cook, houseboy, waterman and wood chopper. In the quiet of the kitchen house they would refer to me as Mrs. Strong Mouth.

My change, turning towards God, or putting my foot on the right path—whatever you like to call it—came about two years after my arrival, in answer, I suppose, to my first honest prayer to God. At the time Alfred and I were by ourselves at Bambili where the Welle River joins the Congo. He was to do translation work and we had chosen this place so as to be undisturbed. Very few of the local tribesmen visited us. I happened to be suffering more and more from indigestion, from endeavouring to eat the food of the country. I really thought I would die. One night I could not sleep and in my despair I said to God, 'Here am I, a missionary; I have left home and friends to come out here and you let me be ill and you don't heal me.' God has different ways of dealing with human souls. The sacramental channels whereby the life of grace is planted in the soul had never reached my heart. Once or so in my life I had felt the touch of God upon me; now an inner voice began to speak. It seemed to say, 'What are you doing? You have been given a pair of hands and feet and you don't use them except for yourself all the time.' After a pause, 'I wonder what you *are* doing?' I replied, 'If I were strong, I would work.' 'Well, get up and try.'

Next morning as Alfred was shaving, I told him what had happened.

'What!' he said, 'you awake all night and not waking me!'

'Well,' I said, 'the outcome of it all is I am going to try and talk about God to one man a day.'

When I had wound up my house for the day, telling the cook to do chicken this way or that, I took my umbrella, for the sun was getting hot and started out to find my one man to speak to for the day. In spite of the scarcity of population I usually found someone, either a man hoeing his field, or a woman fetching water.

One hot day, when I was walking along, a little child followed me, but I had bigger fish to fry and so walked on. I came to a hut where about six or seven grown-ups happened to be having a meal. I had some food with them and began to give my message. When I came out, the little boy was sitting on the verandah listening. He was still trotting behind me when I went home. At last I turned and had a few words with him. Long after, when a mission station was opened at Bambili, a young boy turned up to be the first to join the school. 'Oh, yes,' he said, 'a white lady once gave me the message and I am a believer.'

In the afternoon I would sit and listen. It has been said, 'When man listens, God speaks.' And if, as I believe, God can speak to the human soul through the enlightened conscience, then this was the most direct expression I had of hearing His voice. It seemed in those hours of reflection that my blindness was taken away. I saw myself for the first time as I was before God: first and foremost an egoist, selfish, self-centred, dishonest in small mean ways. If God's command was 'to love thy neighbour as thyself,' then surely I was wanting here. I did not like my missionary neighbours, nor the Africans. In fact, I was trying to do God's work with the tool of an unloving heart.

I began to put things right as far as I could see and, with my obedience to what I believed God was trying to say to me, there came a change. To begin with, if there is such a thing as a sense of God's presence possible to human beings, I experienced something of it then. I felt a new peace and relaxation in the battle of life.

By this time we were back at Nala. Alfred often had to be out on trek in the villages. Always before, I had begged him to come back soon, 'Just one day earlier,' I would ask. Now I wrote to him, 'Don't hurry home, I am quite all right.' And in the evening by the glow of the log fire, with the night watchmen outside clinking their drinkng cups and murmuring, I would sit, the door shut, with my Bible on my knee. I would read by the flickering light of an old Nestle's milk tin filled with palm oil and a rag dip. What peaceful hours they were; the fever of my heart seemed stilled. I was slowly finding what I believe are the only true ways to live this life and work. That inner voice would persist, 'It is no use your preaching about the love and gentleness of Christ on Sunday, while pushing your houseboys about during the week.' 'All right,' I would say, 'show me how.'

Not long afterwards an incident occurred which put that to the test. I went to my storeroom and found two Christian boys helping themselves to the red palm fat used for lighting. They loved to put it on their food. The large native-made pot stood on the floor and they were putting helpings into their enamel plates. Instead of going off into fireworks, I found myself calmly sitting down and watching them. You never saw two fellows more ashamed of themselves. They got up with heads hanging. At last I said, too harshly, considering my own poor show as a missionary, 'You are Christian boys and I thought you had left things like stealing behind you in the water when you were baptized. Now you can take that pot of fat to the kitchen and finish it. I don't want to see it again.' They could hardly believe me. They did not stir. I said it again, 'Take it away. I do not want to see it again.' They walked out, the pot in hand. When they got to the kitchen, they were met by a roar of laughter from the other two boys. I was about to walk after them to say one strong word, when the voice said, 'You keep quiet, I will show you.'

Next morning, no early morning tea came. There was an ominous silence in the house. I got up to see what was the matter. On the back verandah I found four boys, all with very long faces.

I said, 'Whatever is up?'

They said, 'We are all ill.'

After handing out a pill all round, I tried to share with them my experience. They seemed to understand. After that I never had my houseboys so ready and willing to do my slightest wish. There was no more need to shout. One of these boys was with my Father in his last days.

There was yet much to learn. Take the matter of my mud house only. True, it comprised nothing of value but it was *mine*. My selfishness rose like a monster to stare me in the face. I did not want God to have the use of it. I was on a journey at the time. I had not seen my home for three months. The thought came, 'I almost hope a thunderstorm will burn up the whole house before I get to Nala and make short work of it.' Second thoughts were a little more positive. I could anyhow make a beginning in sharing my storeroom. I kept this room locked because of the boys, but in the back of my mind I think I had Alfred as well. He had a way of lingering in the doorway and saying, 'The runner is just leaving for Poko, "So-and-So" has had fever. Let's send him a box of biscuits.' I would let him have them, but with bad grace and say, 'Well, anyhow, don't take the Petit Beurre, take something else.'

I mentally gave God the key, but when I was in there one day I shoved underneath the shelf with my foot the case of butter, most precious of all our commodities. I did hope no one would be needing butter. All of a sudden Nala seemed to run out of butter, so I gave away the butter, remembering something in the Bible which said, 'Give and it shall be given unto you.'

My Mother at home, who knew nothing about it, was given £5 by an aunt who said, 'Buy Edith some stores.' And Mother bought butter. Then she ordered by mistake a second lot. When I left Nala for good and was distributing my stores, I could have swum in butter.

There was one missionary in particular who made me furious. She was the daughter of a doctor. No day seemed to pass but she would ignore me, or show aversion with some marked slight. I naturally reacted to her as she did to me, with an equal dislike. God showed His way to be indifferent to other people's animosity to us and we must not take to heart the hurts and frustrations that we met in our path. We must love friends and enemies alike because He sent the rain on all, the just and the unjust alike. And that equality of love, God's love, not human love, was what I must seek between me and my fellow men.

'What shall I do about her?' I asked. That morning I had read from the Bible, 'And Mary took a box of ointment very precious, and broke it, and gave it.' The idea came to me, 'Send her something of value now.' I can't remember what it was, perhaps just a tin of butter! Anyway, I wrote that verse on a piece of paper and sent it off. In no time at all she arrived with some fresh baked cakes piled on a plate. When we met, all the barriers that had separated us seemed gone before we spoke a word. Actually we said little, but we smiled and thanked each other and there was gentleness and freedom between us. This understanding which came about, like the crack of an eggshell, remained for the rest of the time we were together. The barriers never returned.

One evening when Alfred was away, there came a knock at my door and there stood another missionary, Mary. She had come out from England with her sister. They were girls of character and independence. She sat down and said, 'We have all noticed a change in you: I have come to ask what has happened.' I said that if I had gained anything it was not through some theology or angelic blessing. I had for the first time in my life seen myself, as I was before God, selfish, dishonest, unloving. I had bared my heart to God's estimate of me and had, in so far as I could, accepted His criticism and tried to put things right in the light which I had received. I shared with her such experiences as I had had—no matter how humiliating it was to myself. With a cry of real anguish she got up, opened the door and fled. I found her after quite a search.

'Mary, whatever made you do that?' She came back and said how some word had pierced her heart; she must make it right with another missionary at once. I had hardly known her and her sister, but again this led to an open undertanding between us and a happy working in our daily life.

Three young men passed through Nala. I had known them in England when they were in training as missionaries. They were on their way to Ibambi, some two days' journey south of us, where Father had recently opened a new station. They came in for a cup of tea. At Ibambi they gave out, 'There is a change in Mrs. Buxton. Something has happened to her. She even looks different.'

Some of the elders came next. 'Tell us,' they said, 'what has made you new?'

Again I shared with them some of my adventures with God. With open eyes and mouths they said, 'But, mama, we can understand this! Much of what is preached to us in the pulpit is like a cloud of words. We cannot see through it.'

And so, with a softer tread, I started to walk the path of service with a new and contrite heart. There was much yet to be done in me, a work that would go on to my life's end. But I had made a beginning.

13

ALONE IN THE BUSH

ONE sunny morning I went out after breakfast to join the half-dozen missionaries on the station for the usual daily conference on the work. Alfred read a message from Chief Mafoi that morning. Chief Mafoi was a great handsome man with a bearded face like some Macedonian prince. He had been a baptized Christian for two or three years. He had five wives. Father did not believe in cutting down a man's existing wives because they would be thrown out to become prostitutes. However, the convert had to keep only his legally acquired wives and to promise not to add any more after baptism. Mafoi had done this secretly—married a beautiful girl, who a year later died a most tragic death. His grief brought back to him his promise and he took her death as a sign from God. Calling his people together he made a full confession.

He said in conclusion, 'Do not think you can mock God. Do not become a Christian unless you are prepared to abide by His laws.'

The people were much impressed with these words coming from their Chief. The outcome was, strangely enough, not a turning away from Christianity, but a request from the whole village that the church which had fallen into disrepair might be rebuilt in their midst, and God's protecting presence among them restored.

The question at the conference was: who would go to Mafoi's village, thirty miles away through the bush, and do this work of rebuilding the church? Nzanga, the

Christian who had lived in this village for the past year and had no doubt helped Mafoi through this distressing time, had arrived that morning with the call for help and brought eight porters to carry the missionary and his belongings back.

All around the circle were blank looks—everyone had their jobs to do: the mistress of the school could not be spared; the head of the carpenters could not leave his responsibilities; Alfred himself was up to his eyes in work, and so it went round the circle. No one was free to go—except me. I was hesitant indeed. Once before I had lived for a month in a native village with another woman missionary and we had had a pretty difficult time, with a drunken Chief paying us visits at night. But to go alone! Father had said that in coming out to the Congo we must be prepared to do a man's job. Was I being called to do this very thing? I offered reluctantly to go, hoping Alfred would say at once, 'No, you can't possibly go,' but he was silent. I wandered back to my house feeling now there was nothing for it, but I must go.

That week I had received in a home letter a text chalked by my small daughter, 'Under His wings shalt thou trust.' As I packed, I put this paper on the top of my things in the black box. With four porters to carry the hammock in which I travelled and four to carry the luggage, plus Rukuruma's bundle, two goats to give milk for tea, two goat boys and ten small boys from the school to help teach reading to the bush children, we started off.

The thirty miles was slow going. We left the main track after about a mile and dived into the bush. Bush it was indeed—soon we had to dispense with the hammock; the creepers were as thick as your arm, great gossamer curtains of spiders' webs hung from branch to branch. The tangled undergrowth caught at every corner of the hammock. Soon we were to come upon the goats charging all over the place with the goat boys frantically trying to keep them on the path. At last they thought of a good idea; cutting a pole from the forest, they took hold of each end, and holding it behind the goats' hind legs, they propelled them forward. Plainly, the goats were not liking this journey any more than I was. The going became so slow, with men walking ahead with machetes cutting to right and left, that soon the dark overtook us, and when we came upon a village in the forest we decided to stay there the night.

The village was surrounded by a dense green wall of trees towering above us; the night sky looked down from a great height, dwarfing us all into some ant-like community. The porters quickly swept out one of the small huts, which just held my camp-bed and a couple of boxes. We were all very tired and so made an early night of it. I stood at the door of the hut and looked around before turning in. The schoolboys were eating their supper, curled round a fire. The porters were already laid out round another fire, and Rukuruma and Nzanga were talking quietly like a couple of men of letters across another fire near my door. I looked up at the sky which was like a dark blue enamel plate, studded with stars. I stood gazing as if at the top of a well. I felt closed in, still more so when I shut my door for the night.

My sleep was fitful. No sooner had I blown out the candle and tucked myself in under the mosquito net than, in the silence which had fallen on the village, I heard an incursion of mice invade the hut. They made a noise like trippers on a holiday, rushing, squeaking, fighting, jumping. They climbed the boxes and jumped, only to climb again and jump again. They were having fun. I shone my torch into the middle of the arena and saw two little chaps rolling over each other in mock battle on the floor. They reminded me of a couple of kittens and, with this last thought, I fell into an uneasy sleep. I was glad to see the dawn and hear the porters and schoolboys moving about packing.

We reached the village of Mafoi at about two that afternoon. As we came up the rise I saw on my left the broken-down church; then before me the resthouse where I was to spend a fortnight. There were two rooms, joined by an open verandah. On looking up, I saw with dismay that the roof was only two leaves thick; in fact the sun was pouring through in several places. In those days in the Congo we never dared go out in the sun without our sola topis for fear of sunstroke. So dutifully I wore my sun hat from 9 o'clock in the morning until 5 in the evening, whether in or out of the house.

The missionary's restorative for every occasion is the never-failing cup of tea. Rukuruma had a kettle on in no time and swept in with the tray, but for some reason he left the kettle plumb in the middle of the floor. Over this I tripped, and boiling water poured over my foot, giving me a blister the size of the palm of my hand. Luckily I had a bottle of castor oil, which no missionary would travel without, and I tore up my sheets for bandages. With hat on and bedroom slippers, I must have made a poor picture of an efficient missionary!

Ruku unpacked my camp stuff, hanging the mosquito net, and left me to my ruminations. I felt gloomy as I saw the walls were made of reeds, the small window with reed shutter and door. How was I going to endure a fortnight of this? When evening came, there was a terrific hullabaloo outside and I went out to see what it was. About five men were struggling with one fellow who had come to Nala as one of the porters. He seemed half mad and obviously had been smoking hemp. His eyes were red and bulging and he looked like a devil out of hell. They explained to me above the hubbub that this fellow had stolen one of the wives of a Nala man and they were wanting to know what to do about it. With Rukuruma by my side, I said firmly he must give her up and she must be sent back with the next runner. Whereupon he threw himself on the ground and writhed like a snake. He was forcibly removed and we went to bed.

Two nights after, a strange thing happened which brought me face to face with that creepy darkness of Africa. I knew nothing of it till the next morning when Rukuruma brought in tea. I had heard whispering on the verandah where he slept with the schoolboys, and he looked grave as he told me, 'Last night witchcraft was worked outside this house. Those sleeping in the kitchen saw fire all round the house and there was the sound of the flapping of big birds' wings and the beating of a drum. Someone will die.'

Such signs are all part of the mystery of witchcraft. It seemed a silly tale at 7 o'clock in the morning, the day full of crispness and promise. Presently, the two goat boys arrived, saying that they wished to go home immediately. They were afraid of this death curse. I did all I could to persuade them to stay but they would have none of it and their belongings were already packed. So I sent a note to Alfred explaining, and they left with the runaway wife to return to Nala. I thought nothing of it at that early hour, but by midday I did not feel quite so comfortable. By 6 o'clock I was afraid. It seemed so mysterious and uncanny. We had prayers as usual on the verandah at nightfall, the small schoolboys all crowding round. My Father had taught me, not very successfully, to play the banjo. I knew but one set of chords, so everything had to be sung in this key. I felt the monotony, but not so the boys; they sang their heads off. There was one particular chorus that I remember. It went like this:

Bringing in the sheaves,
Bringing in the sheaves,
We shall come rejoicing
Bringing in the sheaves.

We certainly brought in many sheaves to the thrum of the banjo, but I don't think we brought in any converts.

I said, 'Good night,' and shut my rickety door. The silence of the African night filled the room. In the flickering darkness of candle light I remembered the text 'Under His Wings shalt thou trust', and with my Bible under my pillow I slept sound as a bell until morning.

The days fell into a pattern: a class for the schoolboys in the morning, open school in the afternoon for the village, with a chart of the alphabet which read, B—A = Ba, D—A = Da, M—A = Ma, and so on. The village gathered round, my young school friends leading the lesson in singsong voices, B—A = Ba. They turned their heads in unison, from side to side, to show they really were reading. Listening and trying to hide my amusement, to me they seemed like a lot of puppies barking.

In the evening Mafoi would pay us a visit and bring with him a team of chaps to play ours at hockey. As it grew chill, the immense African night folding us in its shadows, a fire would be lit between two huge trees. The inevitable cup of tea was served. Mafoi liked tea, but when I gave him Christmas cake to sample, he excused himself and spat it out behind the house.

There was, too, the work of overseeing the rebuilding of the church. Poles were cut from the bush and the women brought leaves, carried on their heads in such large bundles they were almost eclipsed except for a pair of feet, and resembled a new species of creepy-crawly. Alfred sent the head Christian of Nala—Baragueni—to visit us and see that we were all right.

When my foot had somewhat healed, Mafoi took a number of us to visit his old father, Chief Gamu. We journeyed for miles along a bushy track and emerged into a huge clearing with a palatial palaver house. Chief Gamu was a regal figure and very old. He reclined on the ground lying on an enormous beautifully tanned hide, cream in colour. His skin was young and oiled, of a pale chocolate shade, his nails manicured, his hair plaited in tiny plaits close to his head and then mounted in a basket-work tiara. I advanced slowly between Mafoi and Rukuruma down the long building as if in the presence of royalty. Then my camp chair was put down in front of him. Ranged like a choir to my right and left behind him were the sub-chiefs, immaculately spruced in oil and bark cloth.

There was silence for a while, then the usual greetings were exchanged. He looked at me out of eyes which seemed to reflect the glamour of an age-long past. I wondered what he had seen and known. Evidently he had been thinking out what to say to me. He delivered himself thus:

'This Christianity which you have come to teach us is good. Is not my second son, Ezeno, in your school at Nala now, learning to read and write? But when it comes to cutting down our wives, this makes it impossible for us to become Christians. Our custom is that the wives do all the hoeing and planting; they fetch and carry water; they do all the cooking. Where should I be without them? My visitors daily amount to a great number. Who would feed them? No! It is not possible for us to become Christians.'

I saw his point. I was up against an age-old custom. I did not have the answer. There was no need to urge him to believe in God.

'We all know Nzambe.'

No necessity to prove to him the existence of an after-life.

'You have only to look at a tree to know that.'

'The Ten Commandments? Who taught you?' I said. 'The white man?'

'Oh my, no, we have known them always, right and wrong is handed down from one generation to another.'

'Sin?'

'Oh, yes, we know sin.'

'What are you going to do about it?' I said. Ah, there I had a point—this time *he* didn't know. 'God's Son came into the world to help us to God.'

And so the talk went to and fro. At last I rose to go, the question still in my mind: could this man become a Christian with 200 wives? I could see his point, too much so, to be a good missionary.

Perhaps that was the last talk we had about these things, for not long after Chief Gamu died.

At the end of the second week the church was completed, the first service held, Baragueni preaching the sermon and Rukuruma giving a word.

The day came to pack up and go. We rose at 4 a.m. so as to be able to make the journey in one day. I arrived back at Nala at about 3 p.m. to find Alfred packing up to leave on a five days' journey to Niangara, where one of our missionaries was desperately ill with blackwater fever.

14

THE UNKNOWING MARTYR

ONCE when Father and Alfred were on trek I visited Deti Hill, an unoccupied mission station two days' journey south of Nala. Titule accompanied me. She was a great big Amazon of a woman, with a heavy jowl. In her former life she was never to be found in the same village for more than one week. She was loud of voice, domineering, and her face showed the depravity of her heart. In a native village, late at night, I had seen her for the first time by the light of the giant fire round which they danced. 'There is Titule,' said the Christian boy at my elbow, 'she is now living with Chief Bodio.'

Next time I heard of her, she had become the wife of one Mabumbe, a good Christian lad, and we all shook our heads and said, 'Mabumbe is a man of much foolishness.' Then she ran away. The young missionary who employed Mabumbe was full of indignation. With the husband he set out one morning to track her down. They found the village where she was. She came out as a young tigress to meet them. Taking the young missionary by the shoulders, she shook him—shook him well—and discretion being the better part of valour, they turned and came home!

But there came a day when she was wonderfully regenerated and marvellously altered. Now she stayed at home: Mabumbe was her chief care; and when I went to visit her in her new house she showed with some shyness a little alcove at the back of the hut—a place portioned off where she could kneel and pray in quiet.

Her passions heretofore so woefully astray flowed down new channels of tender love and sympathy. A white baby died on the station. He was the infant son of my sister, Pauline, who had joined the Mission and come to the Congo with her husband, Norman Grubb. It was two o'clock in the morning. Everything that could be done had been done; and the little company of missionaries sat by the fire and wept. The news spread to the native quarters, and Titule, taking a piece of burning wood to protect herself against stumps and snakes and wild animals, sped along the dark avenue of palms to the white mother's house. She crept into the room. Had it been a death among her own people she would have been wailing wildly. But her new tender heart told her to mourn as the white woman does; and she sat down silently by the fire, laid her big coloured hand on the mother's white one and mingled her tears with ours.

This was the Titule who accompanied me. It was magnificent to see her swinging along the path in front of me, but she had one fault—she turned in her toes!

Arriving on Deti Hill, Titule and I made ourselves very comfortable in a little hut. It was round and made of bamboo. First there came the camp-chair, then a table; after that the big creaking bamboo door; behind it the chop box, the larder box, then my wardrobe box; halfway across the middle of the hut was a screen and behind this was my bed and bathroom. I would take a last look round before going to sleep.

It was the wet season when I was there, but every season had its charm. How the rain would come down and the wind would blow at sixty miles an hour on Deti Hill. We could hear the storm rising in the distance and I would say, 'Titule, make up the fire.' And she would blow out her large generous mouth and in a minute there would be a blaze. We felt very snug and we would increase our snugness by talking of leopards and lions.

One night there was a cry from far away. 'What was that?' I asked. Titule said it was a man warning villagers that human leopards were about—men who would dress up in leopard skins. They would prowl about at night looking for some belated villager to pounce on and kill. They would then take him home, cook him and eat him. Then she rolled up in her blanket and in half a minute was fast asleep, leaving me at the mercy of her bloodcurdling story.

Deti was a place of storms. The thunder would roll round the hill, then a flash of lightning. In a second, sheets of rain would fall. Titule and I would sit and watch from a chink in the door and my arm would steal round her waist and I was glad she was there.

In the morning all was fresh and clean. It was good to be alive. The bamboo door was flung wide open and in defiance of all good custom, I washed and dressed, peeping out on the new world before me. Titule, who had been out long ago, was squatting on the cookhouse verandah, eating a banana. The waterman was in high glee, having left his pails out overnight he did not need to go and fetch water from the stream at the bottom of the hill. He yawned and stretched himself luxuriously. The chickens crowed, the dogs barked, the drums beat, and so the day began again.

One morning while I was there, the lovely view over the roseate top-knots of the palms touched with sunlight —the new day—was suddenly obliterated by a large figure standing in the door. I did not look at his face, my eye did not get further than the mail bag. Now there is one sight that does more good in Africa than bottles of tonic, and that is the mail. I jumped up to receive it, but a reproachful voice said, 'Don't you know me?'

I looked up and then he added, 'Rukuruma.'

'You, Rukuruma,' I said. 'The little school boy who passed round cake at my wedding, who went home to your village and never came back! Oh, Rukuruma!' We shook hands and laughed and then shook hands again. Between the reading of the letters I peeped down at him sitting by my side and slowly I began to recognize him.

He had come to find Alfred and me because he wanted to work for us. From the first he took possession of the whole household in the spirit of an elder brother; he gave us the feeling that all was well because he was there. There was order in the cookhouse from that day forth. Five long years had elapsed since he left Nala School. He had spent them in a heathen village, with its beer feasts, its witchcraft orgies, its murders by poison. He was, moreover, the son of a famous chief, handsome and large-limbed, a man of letters and clothes, a target for the admiration and attention of every Delilah. The contrast from the sheltered life Rukuruma had come to know in Nala School is easy to imagine. The five intervening years about which we did not speak lay like a shadow between us, which disappeared as the days went by and Ruku again found home and shelter for his disillusioned spirit in God.

The day to bake came. The nerve-racking process of baking a cake in a biscuit tin, on a wobbly tripod, with a wavering fire underneath, must be gone through, for we were expecting a visitor.

'Ruku,' I called, 'come make me a fire.' The cake mixed, I set it on the rickety shelf in the oven and Ruku, feeling in his inexperience the worst was over, sat back on his heels and half closed his eyes. But I urged him to watch, putting the bellows in his hand, to be ready at a given moment to blow the failing fire back to life.

'It is a tricky business, this,' he thinks. 'All this palaver just for a piece of food no larger than your hand and gone in no time too.'

Into the hut there stepped another white woman. She sat down and, forgetting the cake, we talked. Do not ask for the conversation; suffice it to say she wept. She was far away from home, no father or mother at hand. The tears were too much for the soft-hearted Ruku. Unable to leave the hut without passing us, he quietly withdrew behind the bamboo partition. An hour passed and he had sat it out without a sound, until my friend left.

Ruku and I did not live without differences of opinion. There was a day when he gave me notice in a very lordly style. I did not say much, but I must have looked like a collapsing balloon, for Ruku stayed.

When Alfred returned, Ruku felt it was his duty to record all that had passed in his absence. We were having our first cup of tea together, after some weeks of separation. Ruku came quietly into the room and closing the door firmly after him stood to deliver himself:

'Bwana, it is good you have returned. During your absence there were several days when all was not well between Mama Bakasi and me. Once before I served a white man, but he was a bachelor and we got along very well. White women are a great puzzle to me, but I think I understand them better now. I find they cry easily and need lots of care and attention.'

Back in Nala, a fine young fellow passed my front door one Saturday. He was well breeched, with khaki jacket, wide felt hat and ostrich feathers. What matter if the jacket was small? The damsels in the market would not notice the belt was almost underneath his arms and that the sleeves were strained to splitting. He patted himself here and there, then turned to see me watching, and we smiled. This was Rukuruma going to buy eggs. Already the Nala market had been humming some hours.

'Hurry, Rukuruma, or all the eggs will be gone.'

But Ruku, of the proud Avongara tribe, was majestic even in his hurry. It was at the end of the day he came to me and said, 'Mama, my father has sent me many clothes. I have a box and padlock but one of these fine market days some wicked man, knowing my wealth, will steal into my house and take my box of clothes while I am buying your eggs.'

The situation was a difficult one. The carpenters were loaded with orders from many stations. White men and women wanting chairs, tables and windows. How could I add another door for Ruku's hut? On the other hand, Ruku might be overcome with sorrow if he lost all his possessions, and return to his village.

'Ruku, you shall have a door,' and hesitatingly I suggested to the boss of the carpenters that a door should be made.

One blazing morning, standing on the back verandah, I peeped through the trees and saw the door was fixed. My sun hat found, I ran down the steps and over the ditch. I reached the door. It was open. There was the famous box of native making, so small, so poor, with the clip made out of old tin. I looked upon the door and the cheap little padlock purchased by Ruku, and my heart was filled with great pity. These were my black brother's earthly possessions. Just behind me stood my own mud house.

The contrast appalled me. How could he ever understand? How could the abyss between us ever be bridged? To him my camp-bed was a luxury, my chairs and tables a fortune, my few saucepans and frying-pan a superabundance. My tin box and other possessions made me a millionaire. I turned away depressed—a hopeless fear in my heart.

Often Alfred and I left Nala and civilization behind and would trek through the forest, visiting out-stations. How easy the road was when travelling with Ruku. One morning an overflowing river confronted us; the obstinate hammock bearers said, 'We cannot carry you through it, we must all turn back.' Eight miles of weary road lay behind us.

I sat down and waited for Ruku. He came swinging along the track, hurricane lamp in hand. This badge of office shouted to all the villagers, 'Here is the white man's boy; he, familiar in all white man's mysteries, gaze upon him, O my brothers and sisters,' and Ruku, with a magnificent air, strolled on, hoping all would see him, but looking as though he did not care a cent. It was soon settled; grasping in his own strong hands the rear hammock poles—a two men's burden—he pursed out his lips towards the river in a manner of pointing and shouted, 'ON!' We were soon in motion; into the surging stream we went. The men were up to their armpits in water, but Ruku piloted us through. However, the trouble did not end there. Every bit of luggage had to be carried through that water, blankets, beds, chairs, boxes, food and the precious foolish things which all humans take with them on journeys. In the evening, the baggage was opened, bedraggled and damp. It was times like that, faced with patience and a cheerful word for the porters, that proved the heroes and heroines; I have seen and known them and felt ashamed.

We had been away at a neighbouring station and were to return to Nala next day.

'Mafuta,' I said, 'make bread for two days' journey.'

It was not one of the cook's best days and instead of a loaf he made a brick. A white woman popped in as he was packing it and seeing the muscles stand out on his arm as he laid the brick in the box, ran to the house and fetching her own white loaf, light as a feather, exchanged it for the brick; and only Ruku saw.

That evening we sat down to eat. Ruku stood at the chop box and held up the napkin which had contained the brick.

'See,' said he, looking as if he were a juggler and we the children, 'See what Mama Renna's done for you,' and then he displayed the loaf as light as a feather.

One day something happened which made it necessary for us to move house to make room for another white couple who were coming. I called the cook and houseboy and told them I wished them also to change their houses and take possession of the ones which were near our new home. They were not in good condition and there were no doors. Three little shanties standing in a row, one for cook, one for Zelada and one for Ruku. But as I stood thoughtfully opposite them I decided, 'No, I will not ask Ruku to change his, I must spoil him again. It will break his heart to leave his wooden door.'

A few hours later he came to me and said, 'Mama, do you expect me to change my house also?' His voice was rather haughty—and I was sorry.

I replied, 'Oh, no, Ruku, I do not ask you to change. You stay where you are.'

We had been in our new quarters some days. One morning I had just finished with cook, having told him to 'do chicken, do potatoes, do greens.'

'How shall I do the chicken?' he had asked.

I floundered among the twenty-six ways of doing chicken and pounced upon one. 'Make koko bifitiki.' (This is chicken camouflaged into beefsteak!)

He departed and I was about to take up my other jobs for the day when Ruku confronted me. It was a different Ruku. He had a softer look about his mouth and eyes. He hung his head, he hesitated.

'Yes, Ruku?' I questioned.

'I have come to tell you something—I have changed my house. For three days I have been in and out of my good house, thinking. In the evenings, sitting by my fire I have cried and my brother has sat opposite me exclaiming, "Ruku, great big fellow that you are, what do you mean by these tears?" I could not tell him. I have come to tell you. I have never forgotten what Mama Renna did for you in giving you the good loaf for the bad one and so I've changed my house.'

The day came when we had to part. Ruku was to go on a visit to his father and then join the missionary at Niangara to help him run the station, and we were to go home to England. He believed this to be the work he should do for God, though he could have earned much higher wages as a clerk in Government service.

The parting was as most other partings. We spoke of when we would meet again. We shook hands, we turned away; we thought of the words we wished we had never said and of the things we should never have done. I looked over my shoulder to see a retreating figure walking down a dusty road and then a blank. We missed him—at the table, on the verandah, in the cookhouse. At the wash-up table on the back verandah the basin was turned upside down as if to say he has washed the dishes for the last time. What did it matter now that he never would use a dish-cloth, but wiped cups, saucers, plates and everything over with his big black hands.

As I packed my trunks for England I came upon a woolly coat. It refused to fit in anywhere; it was brown, it had travelled with me miles and miles in hammocks. It had become naturalized. It could not have faced England again. So I sent it to Ruku, with my parting message. In return a letter came in a large and sprawling hand, 'Thank you, my mother, for the coat.'

After some months he wrote again. 'How is it, my white man, I have not heard from you? We are praying much for you as we hear you are not well. The Scripture says if anything happens to you, look to Jesus. It matters not if death should meet you, look to Jesus. He will save you from all that befalls you. I went to my father's village and he told me not to return here to Niangara, but I did not consent to him. I am engaged to be married.'

Ruku's letters reached us when we were at our cottage in Surrey. One day I had done my chores, working almost unconsciously, for my thoughts were away in Africa. It is a strange thing but Africa does steal hearts. I am sure Livingstone is glad that his heart is buried under that baobab tree. But I was recalled back the three thousand miles by the staccato burr of the front door bell and there was the postman, and a letter from Africa!

'. . . It is with regret that I have to tell you that Rukuruma died on June 9 from poisoning administered by the witchcraft people, while staying at his brother Gima's village.' The letter went on to tell how he had stayed a Sunday at the Mission's little outpost, 'and had given a word in the church, showing an exceptional grasp of the truths of our wonderful Scriptures, quoting passage after passage from the Book of God.'

From there he had gone on to his elder brother Gima in search of his wife, doubtless with another bundle of large iron knives to add to her bride-price. It was at his brother's village that he died, or rather that he was martyred. To begin with, he was in the bad books of father, mother, brothers and his tribe because of his new understanding of God and his persistent refusal to return to the old life. Such a return would have meant great prosperity, for he was to be his father's clerk—the one man of letters in the village. It would be he who would call in the people to receive their tax money, it would be he who would scrawl their names on bits of paper, and be chief barrister in all the tribal squabbles. He again would be the best-dressed man for thirty miles and, around him all the black beauties would flutter.

But he had rejected all the best that his tribal world could give, to discover new truth and to love it. It is difficult enough to stand alone and suffer the disapproval of family and friends in any circumstances or time. It is even more lonely to act with an individual conscience against the strength and cohesion of the tribe in Africa and pay the final price as an outcast. I wept for Ruku and as I wept, the words came to me, 'Blessed are the pure in heart for they shall see God.'

15

LIFE'S GREAT CRISIS

WHEN Susan was nine months old we were due for furlough. After her dedication (a very informal affair with eight other African babies) we packed up for the long journey home by the Nile. A fortnight's trek and then a shaky motor on a very ramshackle road would bring us to the Nile in three weeks all told. I had put Susan on to Nestle's milk and she had done well on it for some time. But now it was after the war and stores were scarce. The Nestle's milk was finished and I was forced to give the child the only other tinned milk I had on the journey. This made her so ill, there came a day when I thought we would lose her. We stopped for one night at a mission station on the way. I asked if anyone had a tin of Nestle's milk and two tins were produced. She recovered almost immediately.

Every station we came to along the road home we begged for Nestle's milk. Perhaps only one tin would be forthcoming. And so we made our way down the Nile to Khartoum asking everyone and everywhere for Nestle's milk. The prolonged anxiety sent me at Khartoum straight to the chemist. Seeing a row of Mellins Food, I said, 'I will take the whole row.' The assistant looked astonished, but we never again lacked food for her.

Clad in a nappy and sola topi, Susan did the sights of Khartoum. I wonder if it was in these early days that she absorbed, all unknown to us, her present love of Africa.

By the time we had got through the Mediterranean,

Susan travelling as a deck passenger, and arrived home, we were ready to leave her in the arms of a nannie whom my mother-in-law had found.

On our arrival home Alfred was in need of a break after such a long spell in Africa, so we did not return for another two years.

Towards the end of this furlough my son Lionel was born. Susan was two and a half and Lionel six months old when we turned our faces for a second time to Congo.

The children were to be left for health reasons with Alfred's parents, in charge of a nannie and nursemaid. It was winter 1921. Our last tea was in the nursery and the fire was lit and the lights were on. My heart had been heavy for weeks at the thought of this parting, so that the details are fixed in my mind: Susan already doing the hostess, offering us jam and cake; Lionel, always a happy boy, gurgling in his chair on the other side of the table. I was afraid to look at either of them direct, but out of the corner of my eye I caught sight of Susan's little arm resting on the table beside me, a fat chubby fist and just beneath the elbow a muslin sleeve edged with lace. I could recall that scene for years after.

By now we were adept at partings and we hurried through the farewell and ran down the stairs. They were peacefully asleep that night as the train rushed through France on its way to Genoa, and to Africa and Nala. But there now came upon me such a catastrophe that I was staggered.

Alfred had been the strong support of my life in Africa. I had been the weak and leaning one. No matter what the trouble, it could always be shelved on his willing shoulders built so squarely to carry responsibility. We had gone down to Ibambi in the Ituri Forest, two days' journey from Nala, where Father had settled in 1922, with a flourishing work much bigger than Nala. We had gone to help nurse Father as he was ill with severe fever. Night after night Alfred had sat up with him, caring nothing for his own utter weariness. Then he came back one midnight and just sat down on a chair by my bed. He seemed too exhausted to speak. I got up and said, 'Here, let me help you to bed.'

It must have been about two in the morning that I was woken by a cry of so horrifying a nature that it pierced my very marrow. I jumped out of bed and, raising his mosquito net, I saw he was in a sort of convulsion. This was followed by unconsciousness. After a while he seemed to breathe more easily. I stood rooted to the ground gazing on the once strong support of my life, the gentle, never-failing Alfred. I saw someone struck down as with a cruel blow, and I felt myself sway with the force of it. I could hardly believe that this was the Alfred I knew, with such quick intelligence, able to work sixteen hours a day, able to eat anything, sleep anywhere, do without anything. For a timeless moment I stood still, then I fled in my nightdress and bare feet to Father's house some two hundred yards away. It was moonlight, so bright that the palms cast tangled shadows, and I could feel the earth still warm beneath my feet.

I woke him. 'Come quick,' I said, 'Alfred is very ill.'

Father took one look at him and said, 'This must be some kind of fit.'

We gave him what we could in the way of medicine and he slept till morning. I got up to another kind of life. Now I *was* alone—distracted and desperately afraid. Alfred did not recover for some days, he was too shaken.

The next night, Father having warned me the attack might come again, I did not undress; I sat by the fire with Nzanga, one of our head Christians. To my cry of, 'Why? Why him, on whom so much of the inspiration and organization of the work depends? Why me? Have I not tried to do your will?' There was no answer. God seemed to have withdrawn behind a cloud of impenetrable darkness. It must have been some time after midnight that, in black despair too deep for tears, I literally fell on my knees beside my chair and said to God, 'Where are you? This is HELL.'

There was no answer. Turning over the leaves of the Bible before me, suddenly my eyes fell on these lines in Psalm 139:

> If I make my bed in hell, behold, thou art there.
>
> If I take the wings of the morning, and dwell in the uttermost part of the sea; Even there shall thy hand lead me, and thy right hand shall hold me.
>
> If I say, surely the darkness shall cover me; even the night shall be light about me.
>
> Yea, the darkness hideth not from thee, but the night shineth as the day: the darkness and the light are both alike to thee.

At first I read listlessly then suddenly one word stood out—it was 'hell.' 'If I make my bed in hell, behold thou art there.'

God had used the same word 'hell' back as I had used it to Him. He was there somewhere in the darkness of that night. In the moments, days, months and years that followed, no other answer ever came.

But the next day had to be faced. All one had told the Africans about trusting God and all that, hit one in the face. How about it now? Being a missionary had surely found me out. How much was true in me? How much veneer? The next sixteen years were to be the test.

We had had six years of complete and happy companionship. After his illness there followed sixteen years of ever-deepening anxiety, sleepless nights, further attacks, though only perhaps two or three a year. Yet you never knew when they would come. Journeys here and there, as far as America, when in dread I would watch the shadow approach and recede, or perhaps rising once again it would strike as with a whip lash. Explanations had to be made to our host and hostess, to which would be added the temporary collapse of the work he was doing at that time and on which everything and everyone depended.

Alfred took it with a silence and courage that was complete. Only that aura of peace he had always carried was more marked, as if he knew of some safe harbour. We hardly spoke of it, we could not. When he knew it had come to stay he faced it without shrinking or fear, and he never allowed his calamity to interfere with whatever undertaking he was committed to. To those who knew him it was his finest hour. He once said to me, 'If this has come to stay, I pray I may die in harness.'

Although we consulted many specialists, it was not till years later that it occurred to a doctor friend that he should go to the Tropical Diseases Hospital. Here, after a week of extensive tests, they found it was a parasite of the malaria group called 'philaria', and that it had penetrated his spinal cord. It was too late for treatment to have any effect.

During these years of testing and endurance, I could only grope my way in a fog of misery and doubt, sometimes seeing only a step ahead. To Alfred had come as complete a victory as could come to any man in such a storm—to me no such triumph ever came. He was stalked by the menacing shadow of this illness for the rest of his life. But he was not busy with himself—only with the work he had to do.

I have never been able to regain those days when I seemed to walk with God in the garden in the cool of the day. I had been offended, often impatient in my trial, sometimes I seemed to die a death to all grace and hope in my very soul. And yet one night, awakened right out of deep sleep, I was suddenly conscious again of that once familiar voice. It seemed to convey to me that God understood, that though I had no money, I had offered what I could, my small gay life and a measure of beauty; and that though I had lost the sense of His presence, He was still there and that He would never forget.

16

AMERICAN WINTER—1927

IT was in the late twenties, during our second term in the Congo, that things began to reach a head between Father and us. Two days' journey lay between us from Nala to Ibambi, but the distance did not mitigate the misunderstandings which had grown up between us. Father had made such sacrifices himself that it was in his nature to expect much from others, and most of us could not keep up with him. If missionaries did not come up to scratch, Father felt we were better rid of them. Alfred played the part of peacemaker and wove in and out between them, often getting caught with blows from both sides.

The same thing happened in cases where African Christians had fallen into sin. Father would demand the necessity of church discipline: Alfred would advocate patience and love. Each was representing one side of the truth of the Gospel. But the differences became severe. They also included strong doctrinal disagreements, not between Alfred and Father, but between Father and some of the missionaries. There were those who held that, once a man was born again, no matter what his conduct was, he remained a child of God. Father would have none of this, but stood foursquare on such Scriptures as, 'Without holiness no man shall see the Lord', no matter whether the person in question claimed to be born again or not. Alfred's own viewpoints were more in line with Father's; but he could see enough of both sides always to be aiming for mutual tolerance and reconciliation.

Father had been trained in law and his letters could be

very severe. On one occasion we received one saying we were disloyal, had not played the game and a lot more. I remember flopping into a chair as Alfred read it out. He looked up and suddenly said, 'Shall I get you a glass of water?' Apparently I was as white as the sheet of paper he held in his hand!

At first, all this was like a wisp of steam from the kettle, and we all looked at one another through the haze, trying to decide on which side this Christian brother or that sister was on. Then it really reached boiling-point. A branch of our work had been opened up in America and seven American missionaries had come out to join us. As the split widened through doctrinal differences, the Americans left and joined other missions.

Then, when Alfred was taken ill in 1925, Father urged us to go home. So at the end of our second term, having been seven and ten years respectively in the Congo we left. I remember on the journey back, by the Nile and Egypt, saying to Alfred, 'I've had enough of this, I don't feel I can go back again.' He took it in silence. One thing he was quite sure about all through his life: he would not be put off his calling by anyone, even his wife. We came home to pandemonium, particularly with the problem of an American Committee and no missionaries!

We retired to the country; Dorothy and her husband lent us a cottage near their home, and there we tried to sort out our problems. From that distant summer, 1926, I remember huge bright clouds over green fields; trees, woods and spinneys basking under a golden sun, the cawing of rooks in the elms. I would linger by the ever-open back door, responding to the fresh English countryside and feeling renewal in every breath I breathed. The girl from the small farm next door came over early with milk and butter. The sound of children's voices was everywhere, for not only were there our own two, Susan and

Lionel, but Dorothy's four next door, as well as Grace's one boy, Ian. There would be tea in the hay field, picnics over the hill, packing as many children as we could into an old pony cart, drawn by a still older pony.

Into these days of peace there came one day to visit us a young American, Donald Fullerton. From the start the children adored him. He took part in all their games, and the battles of King Arthur and his knights were enacted with dustbin lids as shields and poles for lances.

He told us the Committee in the States was up in arms over the split and the loss of their missionaries and it was up to us to go over and help in the making of new plans. It was a shocking prospect, but Donald had come at his own expense and we felt that the least we could do was to take his advice and go and see the American Committee.

The three of us sailed for the States in the autumn of 1927. There was work to be done, new missionaries to collect and a new field for them. We had spent all the money we had and there were no mission funds available. The year we spent in America was, therefore, my first experience in an independent sense of what is often called 'living by faith', or as it has been described 'from God's hand to your mouth'. You never mention a need except in prayer to God, even if the need is just a postage stamp. Miraculous tales of God's intervention can be told by those more practised than we were. Being new at it, I must confess I found it uncomfortable and extremely embarrassing.

We went from one place to another on our speaking tour, with just enough to get us there. On one occasion we were leaving a missionary conference and Alfred got as far as the ticket office at the station without a cent in his pocket to pay for the tickets. Suddenly, a man whom we had met at the conference who could not have known of our plight, rushed forward from the end of the queue and put some dollar bills in his hand. Our journeys were to Philadelphia, St. Louis, Chicago, as far south as Baltimore, as far north as Toronto and the Lakes. We had a heavy schedule of meetings at churches of every denomination. One Sunday we were rushed to at least five churches and Sunday Schools.

Alfred and I would divide the speaking between us. He would speak generally about the Mission and the work, and I told stories of individual lives and what I had seen in Africa. I found most adult audiences are still children at heart; they love a story.

There was a stay in Chicago at the Moody Bible Institute, which my Grandfather's and my Father's money had helped to found, and from which thousands of missionaries have gone to the fields. Here we sat down 600 to meals and we often felt lost in the immense organization. But we were busy with speaking engagements and always there were Americans who were willing to take us under their wing.

One beautiful young woman, the wife of one of the leading families in Chicago, became a real friend. I used to spend days with her in her gorgeous apartment with huge windows looking out on Lake Michigan. One day I arrived at the front door to find a notice pinned on it, 'Typhoid, keep out.' I rang the bell and was ushered in as usual by the butler. My friend met me, her lovely face shadowed by grief. Her young son of twelve, heir to millions, was desperately ill with typhoid. I shared her dismay, but partly for another reason. The immense wealth surrounding me seemed oppressive. Despite such material riches there seemed no answer to such a calamity. I felt helpless, for what could I do when everything had already been done? Then, above the fireplace, my eye caught a lovely old painting of the Madonna and Child. Suddenly, my mind saw a way in which I could help.

'Do you believe in prayer?' I asked.

'Indeed I do,' she replied.

'Well,' I said, 'Let us pray here and now.'

We knelt together, two small figures in the huge drawing-room and asked God to heal this child and make him strong again.

He came through the crisis and was on the road to recovery within a fortnight. Some of those afternoons while he was regaining his strength I spent with him, telling him stories of Africa.

Five years later I was staying with my sister in Essex. We went one morning to Frinton to shop and suddenly I caught sight of a familiar form; her blonde hair and neat figure were unmistakable. I ran after her. It was indeed my lovely friend; she had come over from the States with her son and his tutor for a holiday. They were staying at a hotel in Frinton and we soon made arrangements for them to come over for tennis one afternoon.

The boy of twelve was now seventeen. We were sitting out, watching the game. I turned and asked him if he would like a walk round the garden with me. I had not long since returned from Ethiopia and had an old Ethiopian cross which I wanted to give him. As we talked of those five years ago, I slipped it into his hand and said, 'I want you to remember always that your life was, I believe, given back to you by God.'

During the year we were in the States, many Sundays found us in New York. Here we were able to hear some of America's great preachers. Billy Sunday was the Billy Graham of the day. He had his portable stadium built in every city he visited. This held many thousands of people and was always packed to the doors. We were in the third row so I was able to see everything that went on—there was much to see! I have never witnessed such athletics mixed with preaching the Gospel. It certainly held your attention, though I cannot remember a word of what he said. He travelled round with his own masseur, who kept him in fine trim. He charged around that stage using such physical energy as he preached that I would not have been surprised if he had turned a somersault. He took off his jacket, undid his tie; he sweated in every pore. To end up his appeal, he was literally standing on the chair with his foot on the desk. I loved every minute of it—the veiled sense of humour, the noisy united singing, the sway of a sort of emotion only to be found at a prize fight.

Another Sunday we went down to the Negro quarter of New York. We attended an enormous church, crowded with coloured people. The sidesmen were all in tails, white ties and spotless gloves. Alfred and I were the only white people in the congregation. The singing of old hymns and Negro spirituals was lovely to hear. What a gift the Negro has to touch the heart in sadness as well as mirth. A fine figure of a man preached from the Book of Judges, Chapter 12. It tells the story of a quarrel between two tribes of Israel:

> The Gileadites took the passages of Jordan before the Ephraimites: and it was so that when those Ephraimites which were escaped said, Let me go over; that the men of Gilead said unto him, Art thou an Ephraimite? If he said, Nay; Then said they unto him, Say now Shibboleth: and he said Sibboleth: for he could not frame to pronounce it right. Then they took him and slew him at the passages of Jordan: and there fell at that time of the Ephraimites forty and two thousand.

The preacher said, 'You know how to pronounce the

name of Jesus in swearing, in mockery, in jest; but can you pronounce the name of Jesus in love?'

You could hear the sighs of the people who were moved by the preacher. You could hear their tears, for a woman in the gallery broke down, weeping bitterly. The preacher pointed his finger at her and said, 'Way back home, does your mother know where you are this morning?'

At this mention of home, many were much affected. You could hear groans and cries from all over the building. I felt very moved myself; indeed, in all my life I have never been so hard put to, not to cry in public. A wave of emotion seemed to sweep us off our feet.

Towards the end of the sermon we became a bit calmer, and our attention was distracted by a charming christening party which now entered by a side door. The tiny black head of a baby could be seen in the crook of a woman's arm. Amid more singing the baby was christened, and the congregation regained its composure.

Thinking about home in the middle of New York, walking along with Alfred one day, I said to him, 'They do make too much of us here; we might be royalty. Let's go home before they find out we are nobody at all.'

But Alfred, sensing that it was just a homesick child talking, said firmly, 'Not a bit of it, we've got to find new missionaries and a new field for the American Committee.'

And, as the year 1928 wore on, this is just what happened. A party of three men and as many women joined us; no sooner had this been arranged than a letter arrived from the Congo. Collecting our mail at the post office and seeing Father's writing, we opened the letter then and there, standing on the sidewalk in the middle of New York City, the people passing on either side of us. I felt the excitement of reading one of Father's firecracker letters again, but I saw a look of utter dismay on Alfred's face. The letter said we had been too disloyal in coming to America and that we were not needed in the Mission again.

To Alfred, with his friendly, easy nature, it came as a shattering blow; but never for long was he governed by other people's behaviour. The essence of his nature contained a vision to the fulfilment of which his whole being was dedicated. Challenge, difficulties, obstacles were the very breath of life to him. But fighting his brother men with swords or words was alien to his nature; he would rather risk his life in other ways.

We returned from the States in 1928, and the party of nine missionaries under the leadership of Dr. T. A. Lambie sailed that same year for Ethiopia. Dr. Lambie was already a veteran missionary. He had entered Ethiopia some years previously through the Sudan and up the Sobat River. Here he had opened up medical work on two stations, Sayo and Gorei, under the United Presbyterian Mission of America. He was known to the Emperor and several members of the nobility. He was an ideal leader in every way.

As the Sudan Interior Mission was looking for a new field at this time, Dr. Lambie and the party went out under their auspices. It is interesting to look on the present work of these two Missions reborn and brought into being as the outcome of a broken relationship, and see how things are today.

The Sudan Interior Mission on its Ethiopian Field has forty-three stations and two hundred and seventy-six missionaries. The Heart of Africa Mission[1] (Father's Mission) as it reopened its American branch, out of the total of 1100 missionaries, has nearly 500 of them from the U.S.A. in 28 countries of the world.

1. Now the Worldwide Evangelization Crusade.

17

NEW HORIZONS

THE letter from Father marked the midnight hour of Alfred's life. Separated from the people he loved, cut off from the work he wanted to do, broken in health, a lesser man would have turned to bitterness and disillusionment.

Instead he turned his mind away from the hurt within him and gave his whole energies to accepting a new challenge. From this time for the next ten years he pioneered new territory for other Missions to come in and take over. He returned once for a furlough. He never settled down again to mission life on a station. He had for a long time been thinking about the vast area which comprises the Horn of Africa. This might be said to include Ethiopia, Somaliland and the Northern Frontier province of Kenya. Ethiopia presented a unique problem in that it already claimed to be a Christian country, although the Coptic Church was full of superstition. The other areas were peopled with pagan or Moslem nomadic tribes living in the desert which stretches from the rocky promontory of Guada Fui westward into the Sahara. The Horn of Africa now became the centre of his vision and he set about canalizing all the support that he could muster in this direction.

His first journey in 1929 to Lake Rudolf in Northern Kenya was taken on his own initiative. The money was provided privately through a number of friends. The car was bought in the Sudan for the price of two tusks from an elephant shot by his companion, Hamilton Wilkes. They journeyed round Lake Rudolf, establishing a *pro tem.* mission at Marsabit, which was eventually occupied by men of the Bible Churchmen's Missionary Society. In his letters to me he wrote of visits to Karamoja, Moroto, Lotome. Eventually Karamoja was chosen as another suitable site and this was also opened up later by another mission.

Before he left for his first journey he settled us in a comfortable little house in Norwood with the children at nearby schools.

Alfred had never give away his inheritance as Father had done. My Father inherited on his father's death a large sum of money at the age of twenty-five. The story of the rich young man in the Bible who came to Jesus and asked him, 'What shall I do to inherit eternal life?' had impressed him so much that he felt he must follow Jesus' word literally. 'One thing thou lackest: go thy way, sell whatsoever thou hast, and give to the poor . . . and come . . . follow me.'

He was in China at Chungking when he received the solicitors' letter. At the time he was staying with the British Consul there, and he was able to get his reluctantly-given signature for the granting of Power of Attorney in order to give away the money. Coolly and deliberately, as a business man invests in gilt-edged securities, so Father invested in the bank of Heaven.

It was his public testimony in later years that the hundredfold interest which God has promised in this life was an actual reality. He had received 100 per cent and more in gifts sent to the mission he had founded. Of this money, he and Mother never touched a penny.

Not long ago I held in my hand the counterfoil of the cheque book he used on that memorable occasion. As I looked at the first cheque of £5,000 so boldly penned to the Salvation Army I found no regret in my heart, only a great wonder at the miracle of the act.

On the other hand, Alfred felt his inheritance was his only for his lifetime and to be handed on to his children. So it was with all his decisions. They were always made with a balance between fulfilling his own purpose and his responsibility to his family. When I said to him I could not return for a third spell in Africa, he never questioned it.

His was the true missionary spirit, beside which I could only follow but slowly. Even as I had never been able to comprehend my Father, I could see Alfred and his work only dimly. Everywhere his foot trod he would claim for Christ and His Gospel. The solitude of some of those journeys have been well nigh unbearable. But he had a real love of men, no matter what colour. He would look after those who journeyed with him like his own children, and was amazed that on a wet windy night under canvas he could not persuade his few Africans to share his tent. His self-imposed arduous way of life was all the more poignant because he was not unaware of the good things of life. I remember on our first furlough after the first meal in his Father, Barclay Buxton's house, when the table was all white linen, silver and glass, I found him sitting silent upstairs.

I bent down and said to him, 'What is it?'

He replied, without looking up, 'Oh, I don't know, it's just all that clean white shining table makes me realize something of what it means to be a missionary.' This was the only time he ever referred to it.

While on a pioneer safari to the Lake Rudolf area he wrote, 'Imagine me in a native hut, with the entrance acting as door and window. I am writing on a plank on my knee. My bed is on one side of the hut and round the walls are the boxes. On a little table is a lovely red lily that grows wild here, standing in a Nestle's tin. So I am very cosy.'

His letters were filled with the thrill of speaking day by day in palaver houses, under trees, wherever he could get people to listen. But there were days too, of weariness, when his old enemy of sickness seemed to take over and all past and future were shrouded in the mists of present suffering. Like a shadow he would emerge from this gloom to carry on as though nothing had happened.

Once long ago, an old missionary had stayed with us at Nala. He arrived on a bicyle with a small black box strapped behind him. In this were all his worldly goods. His African boy cycled behind him with a similar box on his rear wheel. He spoke to us next morning and his words fell as light upon 'that small pearl of longing in every human heart'. As he was speaking, his face shone; but looking down I saw that his feet were bare in his slippers. I went outside to think over what he said and there on the clothes line, hanging among his few clothes, was his only pair of socks and one handkerchief with a large hole in the middle, so that there were only the corners to blow on. I remember wondering in my dumbfounded mind if it was necessary to come to this in order to achieve a loving selfless service to humanity? I believe then and there on that day so long ago, I said to myself, 'It is not necessary.' But had Alfred decided otherwise? Spheres of influence and usefulness at home were always turned down. 'It does not enthuse me,' he would say. 'My call is to the regions beyond. The unevangelized tribes fill my heart and vision.'

And so there he was among the tribes of the Northern Frontier, the Rendile, the Taposa, the Turkhana, the Murile, the Suk, the Karamojong, those tribes who wander from water hole to water hole, and Alfred wandered with them. He passed as a small lighted torch in the darkness of their night, vanishing in the light of the day, passing on in his fearless humility, always passing on. Who can tell the worth of this work?

Norman Grubb says in his book, *Alfred Buxton*:

> Such men are the spearhead of progress in human society. They contribute just that touch of originality, genius and creative daring, which saves an army from degenerating into a mere machine, a church from settling into a deadly rut of ritual and routine. There was a strain of restlessness in him which no discipline could wholly suppress. It made him an admirable pioneer. His whole being was instinct with the impulse of creation. But such folk are a difficulty. It is inherent in their methods and activities. If they are necessary they are also uncomfortable! They know it; for misunderstanding and banishment are their portion. Their contemporaries know it; because they cannot contain them in their theologies and 'King's Regulations', and are quick to oppose deviations from the normal in their behaviour and have very grave doubts as to their ultimate value. Alfred, with this pioneer urge, was difficult to contain in an ordinary missionary organization.

But it was with such a background as this that his rock-like character was formed, his strong leadership, his selfless service, always leaving behind him a seal of simplicity, sincerity and humility. With his belongings scattered to the four winds in the Congo, England, Karamoja and Marsabit, there were times when he felt the weariness of constant moving.

What was this man and what did his life add up to? He said of himself, 'Maybe I am a kind of wandering star, filling a gap here and initiating an advance there. After all, that is what Paul did, and who wouldn't be a Paul, even in a microscopic way?'

This work around Lake Rudolph which began in a nomadic fashion, fitting the needs of the people, has now become established in four or five mission stations, one of which contains a hospital. They serve a vast area of scattered people and the hospital is the only medical centre available for hundreds of miles.

While Alfred was on his journeys, my life took a turn into quiet waters and I enjoyed ten years of home life. During this time I did some speaking for our Mission at conferences and among women students.

At the bottom of our garden was a large field with five or six army huts, known as the Missionary Training Colony.

Alfred's brother, Godfrey Buxton, had been badly wounded in the 1914–18 war. Seeing he could not become a missionary himself, he had started this work to train young men for pioneer mission work. The usual run of courses at missionary colleges did not comprise practical training of any kind, and practical difficulties might be the first to confront a man newly arrived in the wilds of Borneo or the Amazon. So apart from Bible study, preaching and teaching, subjects such as building, plumbing, cooking, gardening, elementary medicine and first aid were taught. My Father once said you needed only one inch of theology to one foot of practical Christian living, and he would measure up his arm as he said it. And as another man put it, 'The Training Colony fitted you to fall off a precipice and land on your feet at the bottom with a finger in your Bible on the right text suitable for such an occasion.'

The students used to come up through the garden to visit us for relaxation, a cup of coffee at night and a sing-song at the piano, accompanied by the banging of a tea tray to provide percussion.

One evening, two students told me some fifteen of the men were going to evangelize Piccadilly with tracts and personal talks. The lorry was leaving at 11.15 p.m. Would I like to accompany them and work among the women? Being a born show-off and ready at any time for a lark, I accepted. On arrival, we spilled out in a side street and were issued with tracts. I was told to get on with it and meet them again where the lorry was parked at 2 a.m. As one over-enthusiastic chap gave out that he was going to the nearest café to have a strong cup of coffee, and if he felt 'led' he would get up on the table and preach to the café, I felt glad to be clear of them.

I sauntered in and out of little streets; the only one I can recall is Wardour Street. My first contact was an Irish girl, a gentle, soft-spoken creature. I advanced quietly and said, trying to hide my own embarrassment and not increase her own, 'Would you accept one of these leaflets?'

She at once responded and together under a street lamp I suggested she should read it to me. And in her sweet Irish brogue she read, 'Come unto me all ye who are weary and heavy-laden and I will give you rest.'

She told me she had come from Ireland to join a dancing group; this had eventually broken up and she was left without any support. 'This' seemed to be the easiest way to make money. I told her about a Sister Margaret who took girls like her into her home and then got them repatriated. But alas, the last I saw of her was at a distant corner of the street. She was standing with two men haggling over her.

I wandered on into a wide street with older women talking in twos and threes on either side of the pavement. I went up to two of them and offered a tract. One turned on me like a tigress: 'How dare you! Who are you to think you can come and convert us? Anyway, where did you get that fur collar?' Taken aback at her violence I replied with meekness born of fear, for she had raised her arm threateningly, 'Well, actually it was my Grandmother's muff.' I added, 'Anyway I am no better than you; we are all sinners before God. I have not done what you have done, and you have not done what I have done, but we have all done wrong and we have got to say we are sorry to God.' She seemed to subside at this and she started to tell me her story: 'You see, this is the married women's street. Some men prefer married women. That is my husband there', and a little slip of a man passed us walking in the gutter. He had on a mackintosh and trilby hat and was leading a whippet on a piece of string. 'I was a housemaid at £50 a year, then I married. Two children arrived and there was not enough money. It was no use to go back to being a housemaid on £50 a year, so I came into this business.' She pointed down to a street at right angles: 'You see those young girls. That is their street; they don't know what is before them, they have no ideas of the dangers of this job, the illnesses and so on. You had better go to them.'

I began to realize I had no smart answers, only a feeling of increasing friendliness towards them, so I walked on.

The next person I met was a huge man standing outside a building of some importance, with an ornate entrance. He was dressed in a light blue uniform with, if I rightly remember, pink trappings and silver braid. Obviously he was no figure to fool about with, but before I knew it I had put a tract in his hand. He looked at me in utter astonishment. 'God,' he almost shouted, 'there is no God. Look here, you cannot see Him, you cannot hear Him, nor touch Him, nor smell Him,' and he counted off on his fingers as he said it and, turning away, he shouted to someone scuttling down a side staircase into the street, 'Good night, Doc,' and the figure vanished quickly into the night.

Behind me, beside the curb, there was a large car parked with the chauffeur waiting for someone to appear. I put my head in at the window and said, in rather a disheartened voice, 'Here, would you take one of these?'

He accepted it politely, looked it over and said, as if to himself, 'Yes, my mother taught me to pray; I will read it.'

Wandering on, I came to a lady of generous proportions wrapped in an astrakhan overcoat. She looked at the words on the tract and handed it back and, with sadness, said, 'No, dear, it is too late. Don't waste your time on me. Look,' she added helpfully, 'go over there to those three talking on the other side of the street.'

One was a large squat woman to whom I handed the same little booklet. She passed it to a young girl standing beside her. 'Let's give it to her,' she said in a strident voice, 'she can't even catch a man.'

And, come to think of it, no one had accosted me either, the whole evening.

18

ETHIOPIA

As I look back now, I believe that Alfred's last work in Ethiopia was his greatest, for which all that had gone before had been only a preparation. His learning from my Father, his time alone at Nala, his many solitary journeys, all contributed to this last work.

It was when he was at Marsabit that he wrote, 'Usually of an evening I go out into the cut grass, looking north-westwards to Abyssinia, over the great plain.' Always his vision was reaching out beyond his grasp, always his eye turning the arid wastes into the harvest of the Kingdom. Having been some years in the desert lands of Rudolf, he began to turn his mind towards Ethiopia. 'I have had Addis Ababa as my Rome for the past four years, and now at last I believe I shall see it,' he wrote as he made his final plans to reach Addis Ababa on foot. For this he had to return to Nairobi, where he was met by a note from the bank manager to say that he was overdrawn on his personal account by five and sixpence, but he would be pleased to hear that his brother, Murray, had sent £200 to his credit. This journey was of no small account. It had only been accomplished before by one Englishman in 1915. The way was infested with brigands and crossed miles of waterless desert. He was quite inadequately armed or equipped for this adventure. It was a trek of 700 miles and he accomplished it in thirty-six marching days.

Arriving in Addis Ababa, he made himself known to

the British Minister and his wife who, from that time on, took an interest in his work. Without seeing an inch in front of him, he started a Bible class on Sundays. At first it was attended by one Ethiopian, but in a month there were twelve. It was from among this number that the first Ethiopian leaders of the work were to emerge when he returned a year later.

The missionary community wondered why he was coming to start a new work when they were already there; but in spite of their not understanding, nevertheless 'he won their hearts and affections and they were all on the station platform to see him off,' wrote a friend of his departure, as he left after a year's work to go to England to find recuits. He had been away three and a half years.

The year 1933 he spent at home. One Sunday afternoon, we walked together to the local shoe shop as Alfred needed a pair of shoes. The question came up whether they were to be brown or black. With the shoes lying on the floor between us he suddenly said, 'I think I'll have the brown; they will do better in Africa.'

He had been making preparations for this new work in Ethiopia, but I had failed to realize that he was planning to go so soon himself. I looked at him in astonishment and neither of us said any more till we got home. It was just like that, that he would feel an urge to return to Africa. Something deep within him drew him back like a magnet. His was no mere superficial fascination for Africa, but a challenge to adventure which became a driving purpose. It was impossible for him to resist. He was like a man who hears a bugle call and must return to war.

This last year had been a busy one. Going up and down the country speaking about his possible work in Ethiopia, Alfred had collected a fine band of young men and women willing to go. They had been in and out of our home and I knew most of them very well. Yet it came as a surprise to me when we got back home that day and he told me he was not only going to Ethiopia himself, but would like me to come too; he needed me to set up a home for them in Addis Ababa. I had not been to Africa for at least ten years. I did not want to go, but Alfred's insistence that he needed me and the Easneye Buxtons' offer to look after the children overcame my resistance to the idea.

All the same, I went reluctantly. The party consisted of a remarkable set of young men and women. Among them were two young doctor brothers not long qualified from Bristol University, two Cambridge undergraduates, a young girl from a well-known Kenya family, and a man who left a position on the Paris Bourse to join the party. Another young fellow had his own private aeroplane and a comfortable life before him. Then a friend, Caryl Cobb, joined us, coming at her own expense, and a young cousin of Alfred's, Adrian Buxton from Easneye, did the same. There must have been about eight or ten of us and we sailed away in two parties in 1934.

Alfred now used again all the experience which his life in the Congo had given him and the years alone in the Northern Frontier of Kenya. A compound was found in the Ethiopian quarter of the town consisting of three houses. The buildings had fallen into disrepair. They were so dirty that our Ethiopian houseboys refused to clean the houses, so we women, with pails and scrubbing brushes, got on our knees and proceeded to scrub the floors, singing as we went. The houseboys crowded the door to watch us. They were soon doing their share.

We were joined immediately by four young friends of Alfred's who had been in his Bible Class on his previous visit, educated Ethiopians who spoke excellent English.

These four young men of high standing in the country had surrendered position, salaries and lands to give their lives to preaching the Gospel. One, Haile Gabriel, had been Sub-Governor of the Province of Harrar. Two others, Werku and Abeba, together with Haile, had been selected by the Emperor for their intelligence and sent to Egypt for further education and were working in a Government office. The fourth, Tomasgn, was a member of the ruling class, an Amhara from Gojjam, the son of a priest and himself trained in the priests' school.[1]

These four young men occupied one house. Alfred and I and the young women lived in another and the bachelors in a third. The houses were in simple Ethiopian style, set around a large central courtyard with blue-gum trees here and there. Outside the fence were more blue-gum trees and Ethiopian dwellings clustered around. The place had a rural atmosphere. The morning would begin with the two young Ethiopian girls drawing water at the well. Then there was the busy work of the day, coming home to supper all together, with the soft light of the kerosene lamps, the doors shut, and outside the whoop of hyenas like schoolboys on the run as they cleared up the garbage of the town.

It was here I was to live the happiest months I can remember. There was a delightful family feeling. Alfred was like an elder brother to all. He worked *with* the Ethiopians, not *for* them. He would open the front gates every morning and preach in English, interpreted by one of the young men. Quite a crowd would gather from the road outside on their way to work. On Saturdays, in the evenings, we kept open house for anyone who liked to come in. We taught them our games, they taught us

1. *Alfred Buxton*, Norman Grubb, Lutterworth Press, 1942.

theirs. The party would end with evening prayers.

The Europeans warned us about the risk of settling in an Ethiopian quarter, and true there was an open drain running alongside the fence by the kitchen, which was used for the sanitation of the neighbourhood. Maybe it was risky, and in a few weeks half of us were down with dysentery, but we had determined to live among the people and not let a gap develop between us. We made our mistakes, but we made right what we could, and had the kitchen and dining-room wired in against flies. We had our failures too. Many came to ask questions and, counting the cost, turned away regretfully.

We had a Bible school of twelve young men, including two monks and a priest. Alfred took Bible readings, Wynne lectured on Bible subjects and Cuthbert taught a class in English. The students lived in a low building at the end of the compound. They slept in a row on a raised shelf. One night a student feeling that he had let himself in for more than he bargained for, decided to escape. Having no money, he crawled along the row of sleepers at dead of night and, as he had no knife either, proceeded to bite the leather purse off the belt of his sleeping companion and, opening the door, made out into the night.

We were not a united party when we arrived. We had to learn to live together. Some of us disappointed each other, some of us did not like each other. But there began to grow among us, centred round the person of Alfred with his Christ-like character, a love and unity which transformed the difficulties of personal relationships. This new atmosphere began to draw the Ethiopians into our family circle, knitting us together in a strange land.

One evening Werku, one of the head preachers, appeared in Alfred's room and said he had something important to say to him. Sitting on a low stool, this proud young Ethiopian told us that since he had become a

Christian he had had to separate from his wife. She was of the strict Coptic Church, while he felt he had found a better way. The rift had come as much from his own fault as hers. He had not been patient with her and had often walked out in anger. As the days went by on the compound, he felt new light had come to him about the matter. He must go to her and tell her he was sorry, even though this was hardly the thing for an educated Ethiopian man to do. We listened quietly. We were very touched and told him he must do what he felt was right. When he did go to his wife, he found it was as if she had been prepared for his coming. The rift had been so wide, yet as they sat together he felt as if she had come within the touch of his hand. With no few tears on either side the quarrel was mended; he brought her to the compound and she became one of the family.

The three head Ethiopians came one day and offered us a piece of land which three of them had bought together. It was valuable land, for it was by a healing stream to which people came to bathe. The three of them offered it to the mission so that we could build a small house on it for the weekend, to get away from the high altitude.

Alfred had no intention of starting a new church or of bringing Christians into the Church of England. He acknowledged the Ethiopian Coptic Church as one of the oldest Christian Churches in the world and he not only worked through the young Ethiopians, but through their own church. So on Sunday mornings he and the young men would start off with the Ethiopians to the Coptic service in the old Gorgis Cathedral. This ancient church, standing in the middle of the town, was built of weathered sandstone. It had a copper dome and was of a circular pattern with turquoise-coloured doors at all four points of the compass. Here every Sunday morning a colourful crowd of Ethiopians flocked in their white jodhpurs and shammas.[1] Ladies like soft white doves gathered round, wearing white homespun gauze gathered like a sari. Their hair was tied up in stiff black net and they were beautiful to see, with their small neat faces and black almond eyes. Priests in their accoutrements and large coloured umbrellas, heavily embroidered with gold, added to this gay throng. Alfred and the young men, both Ethiopian and English, would take their shoes off at the door and sometimes kneeling on the stone floor, sometimes standing for two to three hours, they would listen to the service conducted in the ancient language of Geez, of which ordinary people no longer understood a word. Alfred felt strongly that this most ancient church in Christendom still had sparks of life in it which should be revived. New life would come to the church, he believed, when priests and people could read the Bible and understand it. It became his central purpose, therefore, to get the Bible read in Amharic (the language of the people) in the churches. The work of translation of the Bible by monks and priests was begun some years ago by order of the Emperor and finished during the time that Alfred was in Addis Ababa.

There came a Sunday morning when the first move to achieve this was made. Haile Gabriel, the leader of the four Ethiopian preachers, had a commanding presence and an eye without fear. Getting up from among the kneeling people, he made his way to the lectern and opened his own Amharic Bible bought from the British and Foreign Bible Society shop in town. In a firm voice he read to the astonished company in a language they understood; and for the first time the Bible story was comprehended by the people.

Their attendance led to the priests seeking them out

1. Homespun shawl.

and coming by night to Alfred. But this success was not without opposition from the conservative element in the Coptic Church. In spite of this, invitations to preach after Sunday service in the precincts of the Cathedral were frequent. Some 300 would be present to listen to these talks. Alfred was always in the background, and the four young Ethiopians became the mainstay of the work. Requests too came from the country to preach in outlying churches. There was an offer to open a new station on the estate of a wealthy Ethiopian nobleman. Invitations came to hold open-air meetings in the town. These would be attended by crowds some 200 strong outside the post office, sometimes remaining in the pouring rain to hear the men speak. They then procured a hall where anyone interested at the open-air meetings could come and learn more.

Life was not all work on the compound. All the missionaries bought ponies, which were quite cheap, and they would ride into the town to do their shopping and meet their friends. Invitations would come from the British Legation to join in a paper chase on horseback or to attend an evening party. Then there was a gathering of the Europeans once a week in different houses. From these outside events we would all return to our home refreshed.

Alfred and I were invited to dine one night at the Emperor's palace. I had no evening dress, but somebody lent me a simple wedding gown and a pair of shoes too large for me. In these I practised as best I could the curtsey which had to be made four times. The nights were cold and at the last moment I found I had no evening coat. I snatched a blue and gold Japanese kimono from the end of my bed. It had been made for me by my sister. No one knew that I went to dine with the Emperor in my dressing-gown.

From the beginning the work went with a swing and

towards the end of the first year it began to reach a crescendo. The four preachers became famous up and down the country. Coming from the educated class, and bringing a new message to so old a Church, they created a particular impression. Though Alfred continued to work behind the scenes, some of the leaders of the Coptic Church sought him out privately to discuss how they could bring back a live faith into the Church.

For some years Italy had had her eyes on Ethiopia to annex her as a colony. No nation came forward to shield Ethiopia from the intruding enemy. By July, 1935, the war clouds were lowering on the horizon. They grew with alarming rapidity. Adrian Buxton and Carol Cobb were leaving for home, their year of voluntary service being over. I took the opportunity of going with them. At the time I felt strongly I should not leave, yet I went. During these months of suspense thousands crowded to hear the preaching with signs of fear and growing emotion. It is difficult to assess how much in those last days the apparent response was due to fear of the imminent upheaval of war. There came a day when the storm broke and it was as if a flash of lightning cracked suddenly across our 'porcelain world'. In the confusion which followed, the city was given over to looters and bandits.

The whole European population was in danger of being massacred. When zero hour struck the Ethiopians foiled themselves by being so drunk on the loot that their well-laid plan came to nothing. Alfred and his Ethiopians ultimately took refuge in the British Legation, but even this was not without loss of life, and Werku's wife and her brother were shot dead. Alfred was wounded in the leg. Another casualty was John Melly, a gallant young doctor who had organized and collected money for his own unit, had come out under the Red Cross to help. He was out in the town collecting wounded when a stray bullet caught him in the lung. Now he lay dying at the British Legation. Pandemonium reigned until the Italians marched in to take the city.

During the riots the Emperor left to put his case to the League of Nations, but first he called Alfred and entrusted him with a Bible. It represented years of work, for it was a translation from Geez into Amharic which had just been completed by the monks. It had been laboriously printed by hand on parchment, the Geez on one page and the Amharic opposite, making a huge heavy volume. This precious but hefty tome Alfred succeeded in secreting out of the country.

When the Italians entered and had quelled the rioting, there was a time of comparative peace when it seemed that the work could go on again. Having received a promise from Marshal Graziani that there would be religious liberty, they went back to the compound and started afresh.

The storm seemed over and for a moment life returned to normal. But in fact the storm had only circled to come back again. On a feast day, when the Italian Viceroy and several high officials were present to distribute money to the poor, suddenly from the crowd bombs were thrown, badly wounding the Viceroy and several of his entourage, though no one was killed. Ruthless action was taken by the Italians, resulting in the worst massacre known in Ethiopia. Hundreds were shot down in the streets and houses were fired. Thousands were arrested and shot without trial and about fifty of our own men were among those who lost their lives. Werku was one of the last to go. He was arrested and shot the same evening. The last that was seen of him was on a lorry going towards the hills outside the city. The city was like a burning torch lighting up Werku's face as he turned to face his executioners. But soon he was to enter that city which hath no need of light, whose builder and maker is God.

All missionaries now were ordered out of the country and darkness descended on the work that had been the beacon light to so many. Everyone was chased and scattered and arrested. Perpetual night seemed to settle on the once happy compound. To those who were forced to leave at this moment of extreme trouble and suffering, their grief seemed too great a load to bear.

Alfred had left a few months before this further catastrophe. Following the Bible which was so dear to him, he had hurried back to England to collect money and arrange for its printing. It was one of his greatest griefs that when calamity had overtaken his Ethiopian friends he had not been among them. Unable to return to Ethiopia, he settled down to two years' work in England, which resulted in the printing of 300 copies of the New Testament which three years later were ready to return to Ethiopia when the Emperor himself went back. A revised translation of the Emperor's Bible into Amharic was made later which bore the following inscription:

> This Bible is given to you from money collected by Alfred Buxton in order to print in Amharic the Bible, which had been translated by Ethiopian scholars at the command of His Imperial Majesty Emperor Haile Selassie. Now by His Majesty's energy the translation has been revised and printed, and this copy is given you in memory of Alfred Buxton, a servant of Jesus Christ, who loved and served the people of Ethiopia.[1]

Among the Emperor's retinue the most outstanding of

1. The latest news of the Ethiopian Bible is from David Stokes, Nov. 1966: 'The Buxton Bibles are out. They are in every district now, waiting for the Holy Spirit on them to bring life to the dry bones of the Church of Ethiopia.'

Alfred's companions was David Stokes. He returned on military duty in the British army to free Ethiopia and later was to carry on the work. The first thing he did was to take possession of the old compound in Addis Ababa and gather together those who had survived.

19

COURAGE TO LIVE

WHEN Alfred eventually returned to England in 1936 after the Italian invasion of Ethiopia, we went to Devon where a friend had lent us a house on her estate. Here we stayed three and a half years, so he was able to have a much needed holiday and time to collect the money to see the Emperor's Bible through the press. After Alfred's wanderings it was a new experience to settle down to country life as a family. Susan and Lionel had now reached the ages of 20 and 18. They joined the not-too-serious local hunt, and on one famous occasion Susan brought home the mask.

Our friend wanted us to settle down, but Devon could not hold Alfred. As soon as the work on the Emperor's Bible was finished, he attached himself to the National Church League to do some work for them. We took a flat in Tufton Street, Westminster, and it was there that we heard the declaration of war with Germany that fateful Sunday morning in 1939. In 1940, having spent two weeks of nights in the basement when we had bombs on every corner of the block of flats, we let the flat to a V.I.P. and removed some of our things to a friend's house at Reading. Here Alfred spent an uneasy weekend and went back to London on the Monday, with the excuse that he must tidy his writing desk for the V.I.P. to use. I urged him to spend the night with his parents in their home outside London. But his brother, Murray, who had to be in London on business, rang him up and asked him to dinner that evening. It was like Alfred that he would not leave him. He cancelled his safe bed and stayed. It was while they were in committee at Church House, Westminster, with four others that the bomb fell and they were all killed. It was the night of October 14, 1940.

> Without belittling the courage with which men have died, we should not forget those acts of courage with which men have *lived*. The courage of life is often a less dramatic spectacle than the courage of a final moment; but it is no less a magnificent mixture of triumph and tragedy. A man does what he must—in spite of personal consequences, in spite of obstacles and dangers and pressures—and that is the basis of all human morality.[1]

I spent half my life with two men of courage who were devoted to God, to each other and to their fellow men. Both did a great work for God, though they did not agree. Yet God stood by each as though not taking sides. God even seemed to bring good out of evil, enabling them to fulfil the work which they each felt He had given them to do; even by their diversity making the Gospel go further round the world.

When my Father sailed with Alfred in 1913 it was said of them, 'One is too old, the other too young.' Small wonder that Father nicknamed the two of them 'Balaam's ass and Noah's dove'. Who would dream that the broken-down ex-cricketer, with malaria fever and asthma, could achieve such a work in Africa, except God was with him? The Heart of Africa Mission began to spread in Father's lifetime until it has become a world-wide crusade.

Father's last year, 1930, was a busy one, though his health was failing. The language in the Ituri Forest was

1. John F. Kennedy, *Profiles in Courage*, H. Hamilton, 1965.

not Bangala as spoken in the Welle Province, but Kingwana. At 70 he mastered this lingua franca and was able over the years to help considerably in the translation of the New Testament, the Psalms and extracts from the Proverbs. The New Testament was a deliberately simple translation so that any of the forest dwellers who had learned to read could take it back to his village and understand it. In 1928 he was working eighteen hours a day. As the translation work finished he grew weaker and heart attacks set in.

At this time he wrote a letter home which gave his last backward look at the outstanding events of his life.

> As I believe I am now nearing my departure from this world, I have but a few things to rejoice in; they are these:
>
> 1. That God called me to China and I went in spite of utmost opposition from all my loved ones.
>
> 2. That I joyfully acted as Christ told that rich young man to act.
>
> 3. That I deliberately at the call of God when alone on the Bibby liner in 1910, gave up my life for this work, which was to be henceforth not for the Sudan only, but for the whole unevangelized world.
>
> My only joys therefore are that when God has given me work to do, I have not refused it.

For nearly twenty years Father lived in the heart of Africa, though at the time he set out in 1912 the doctors had threatened him with death if he returned to the tropics. His work in the Congo was acknowledged openly in Belgium. In 1930, Father was made a Chevalier of the Royal Order of the Belgians by the King of the Belgians for his services in the Congo. And in 1931, in the Ituri

Forest where he had once been entertained by cannibals, he died. He died the good soldier he had lived, surrounded by the African people he loved and whose lives he had done so much to change.

It was a stormy day when they laid him to rest. Two thousand people from the surrounding forests came to his funeral, including Chiefs Kotinaye, Owesi, Abaya, and Simba. Rain poured down. The Africans were shiny with wet in their nature's brown skins; the missionaries had dripping macs and umbrellas. Even the great forest trees bowed their heads and dripped. But the storms of his life were over. They laid him to rest in peace and in solitude. Seemingly his work was done, but Alfred thought otherwise and wrote of him:

> C.T.'s life stands as some rugged Gibraltar—a sign to all succeeding generations that it is worth while to lose all this world can offer and stake everything on the world to come. His life will be an eternal rebuke to easy-going Christianity. He has demonstrated what it means to follow Christ without counting the cost and without looking back.
>
> C.T. was essentially a cavalry leader and in that capacity he led several splendid charges. Three in particular stand out: when C.T. and Stanley Smith led forth the Cambridge Seven to China in 1885; ten years later when C.T. toured the American universities at the start of the Student Volunteers; and when in 1910 he initiated the campaign for the region between the Nile and Lake Chad (the largest unevangelized region in Africa at the time).
>
> These three things alone have affected missionary history and through them C.T. forwarded evangelization to an extent that we cannot properly gauge. These

were his direct work, but the indirect influence which he exerted and which extended in ever-widening circles round the world probably accomplished even more. He impersonated the heroic spirit, the apostolic abandon, which it is easy to lose from the work of Christ.

The cavalry leader cannot have all the gifts of an administrator, or he would not have the qualities necessary to lead the charge. In this simple fact is the explanation of the shortcomings some might point out. If there were these, they were in reality the exaggeration of C.T.'s unique qualities; his courage in any emergency, his determination never to sound the retreat, his conviction that he was in God's will, his faith that God would see him through, his contempt of the arm of the flesh and his willingness to risk all for Christ.

But these are only as Froude wrote of Carlyle, 'The mists that hang about the mountain.' Men who want no mists must be content with the plains, but give me the mountain! It will be but a little while, and, the mists evaporated, the mountain will stand out in all its grandeur.

I myself owe an enormous debt to him. From him I learned that God's ideal of a saint is not a man primarily concerned with his own sanctification; God's saint is 50 per cent a soldier. So we and thousands more will continue to thank God for the soldier life he lived and the soldier death he died.

His life story by Norman Grubb (son-in-law) was published in 1933.[1] That same year a letter appeared in *The Times*, signed Edward Lyttelton:

1. This book is now in its twenty-third edition and has been translated into ten languages *C. T. Studd—Cricketer and Pioneer* (Lutterworth Press).

> I have just read the thrilling memoirs of C. T. Studd, the great cricketer and pioneer of mission work overseas. The reason why I ignored the arresting record of an old schoolfellow was that I gathered that he presented a religion quite different from that which we Cuddesdon men learned from Charles Gore. Nobody of the Tractarian school ever mentioned such fervent ambassadors of Christ except to criticize them as emotional, unsacramental and purely individualistic. The criticism was true; but Studd was a hero saint ... My conviction is that as Catholics believe all that is sound in Protestant teaching—not their details—we ought to look on these revivalist conversions as foundations on which we can build.

It has been said 'Anyone can be brave once, it is sticking to it that counts.' Alfred had that stickability. He had every reason to retire from mission work when his malarial illness came on in 1924. Still more so when Father gave him his *congé* in 1928. But he was no deserter.

The years that followed were spent in journeys to Africa, lasting three years and two and a half years respectively. He took the opportunity of visiting my Father on each of these occasions, travelling thousands of miles out of his way to do so. On these journeys one or two men accompanied him who knew of his ill-health. On the last journey from Nairobi to Addis Ababa he was alone with his African servant and muleteer and a train of mules for the baggage. It was a journey of some months. He fell in with a Mohammedan for some of the way. They travelled together, had their meals together, camped together. Alfred told me of his shame when a beggar came to the edge of the verandah in filth and tatters and the Mohammedan had immediately got up and given his whole plate of food to him and gone without himself.

A friend who had known him and his brothers since boyhood told afterwards of the visit Alfred had paid him a few days before his death. Lord Caldecote[1] wrote:

> His life was an answer and a challenge to the rationalist whose operations are bounded by sight. His faith was a simple one and was never shaken. He believed in the authority of the scriptures, the centrality of the cross, the necessity of the new birth. Yet his liberality had no hesitation in finding the unity of the essentials in diversity of ritual doctrine. In this sense he was the broadest of broad churchmen. Who can say that his example is not pointing the way to a new approach to the problems of evangelism both in the home and in the mission field?

His closest friends after his brothers, Murray and Godfrey, were his two brothers-in-law, Gilbert Barclay and Norman Grubb. Norman summed it up thus:

> I could not get away from all that I owed to Alfred. He was much more than a brother, a friend with a peculiar quality of love, which bound me to him and which has been unique in my experience. During those twenty-two years he has left a permanent impress upon my life. My love and admiration increased as I lived and worked with him in the Congo. I saw the same manifestation of that love towards the African. As years passed, we differed on some major points, but nothing ever overshadowed that changeless love. In his letters there was that same spirit breathing unchangeable through the fresh expression of opinion on men and matters. Agonies, yes, and misunderstandings, the

1. Viscount Caldecote, P.C., C.B.E., the Lord Chief Justice of England, 1940–46.

battles and wounds of mind and spirit which all endure who enter the lists for God, but there was always love. My memories of him, of the real Alfred, are the divine calls, the hesitations, the calculated hazards; the gallant plunges of faith, the storming of the walls that reach unto Heaven; the setbacks, the return to the charge. He taught me to live insatiably, live persistently for Christ and for a world that can find no other Saviour outside of Him.

In the years of Alfred's illness I knew no light to break in upon my darkness. Then at his sudden death, and only then, did I feel that touch of God upon me again. I had known apparent desertion by the very God who had seemed a familiar friend. I felt He was trying to tell me though so long silent, He had been here all the time. As for this—it was best this way. He had done what He had in love. We had always feared that Alfred would have to be taken care of by others. This way we were able to care for him to the last. Now he was safe.

It was in 1942, two years after Alfred's death, that I received this letter from Addis Ababa. David Stokes wrote:

I am actually writing this from our old compound in Addis Ababa which I took over a week ago. Last Sunday we had our first meeting. Most of the survivors of our boys were there. Abeba (one of the original four preachers) led the meeting and spoke first. He told of his prayer in prison that God would grant him that he might just once more stand in that sacred spot down in the big room in the lower house and once more proclaim the name of the Lord. After that he desired that he might die. That prayer, the first prayer at any rate, had been abundantly answered. Then came old Ato

Quana with the shining face; and Emanuel from the Swedish Mission; and lastly Mrs. Haile Gabriel. The name of Alfred was very precious to us there (will you believe me when I say that there are few of us who can speak his name without tears). He was evidently a man greatly beloved and for a few minutes we wept for the master that had been taken from us. We knew—and I who must stand in the breach know as deeply as any—that the gap could never be filled. We felt unutterably bereft. But we are called to build, the strength is God's and we must up and do.

From this day the work grew back again until even the Army and Ethiopian Government officials were asking for 'the Buxton boys' because they were to be wholly trusted.

Not long ago my daughter, Susan, and Michael, her husband, visited Ethiopia, flying over the blistering desert where her Father had marched through long months. She met many of the Christians he had known, among them Mrs. Haile Gabriel who was then in charge of the nurses' home at the Princess Tsahai Hospital. 'She took out her beautiful white lace handkerchief and cried into it for Father,' wrote Susan. 'She loved him so. She said, "He taught me how to live through the troubles of life." '

Susan visited the compound and stood in the room where we had met so often and which had seen so much of the triumph of the early days and the subsequent tragedy. 'I looked out of the windows on to the spindly little green trees outside and thought of you both,' she wrote to me after this visit. 'I read that morning from *The Reversal of Human Judgment*; it said, "I am against bigness and greatness in all their forms, and *with* the invisible molecular moral forces that work from individual to individual, stealing in through the crannies of the world like so many soft rootlets, or like the capillary oozing of water, and yet rending the hardest mountains of man's pride, if you give them time." And I felt the roots of Father's work doing just that.'

Her final visit was to the Emperor himself. He sat behind his big desk resplendent with golden lions, his frail hands clasped, his face moulded by suffering into the austere lines of an Ethiopian saint. Susan asked him if he remembered her Father. And in reply he gave perhaps the best epitaph of Alfred's life, 'How could I ever forget?'

Lionel from early years had been an independent boy with originality and a strong sense of humour. When seven years old we were staying with my sister, Dorothy, who always kept open house, and we must have been sixteen for lunch. It was the day of the Grand National, and another great event had been the return of a dog from the kennels where it had been cured of some trouble. Getting up and facing the table Lionel said in a pompous voice, 'To celebrate the return of Ponto from the vet, I think we should all rise and sing the Grand National.' He went to Cheam School and then to Stowe, and from there straight to his uncle's firm, who were engineers in constructional steel.

When war broke out in 1939 Lionel joined the Royal Engineers and was sent up to Yorkshire, as he put it, 'to learn to dig graves'. Hearing the 3rd Battalion Coldstream Guards were on the look-out for young men, he applied to join them, was accepted, and transferred to the Guards' Depot, Caterham. Knowing that they did everything there at the double, I asked him how he liked it. 'Oh, it's child's play,' he said, 'after digging all those graves.'

The time came for his departure for the Middle East.

The last ten days I spent at the Goring Hotel, so as to be near him. He stood talking with friends from the Regiment in the hall. I remember thinking that their backs were as straight as steel—as straight as Edward III's sword hanging in St. George's Chapel.

In 1942 the 3rd Battalion was sent out to Beirut, and after that to Cairo, from where they fought their way along the African coast. Some months later they landed at Salerno where they were engaged in an uphill battle with the Germans.

I had returned to Dartmoor and was staying with my friend, when one day I received a cable to say Lionel had been wounded. It came as rather a relief that he was anyway out of the fighting. Then suddenly Susan phoned that she had a week's leave and was catching the last train to Newton Abbot that night.

As I leaned over the bannisters and saw her face as she came up the stairs towards me, I never guessed the news she carried. We walked slowly into the spare room where a fire was burning brightly. It was late September, 1943, and it can be cold on Dartmoor. We stood leaning against each other, looking into the fire.

Then she said very gently, 'I expect you know why I have come?'

Trying to parry the blow, I said, 'No, not Lionel?' And she said in almost a whisper, 'Yes.'

My eyes strayed to the long bow windows where the curtains were closely drawn against the bombing. But my mind's eye saw the fields, twenty-five miles of farm land stretching to the Channel. No sign of town or village. Here and there a farm house dropped like a match-box on the grass. The sheep with their lambs would be grazing in the field below. He would never look on this scene again.

No further words were needed, the wound for both of us had been too deep. I was dressing next morning and I remember putting my head in at Susan's door and saying, 'Susan, I feel that in the night someone has spread balm all over my wound.' It was followed by that calm assurance that God had done it in love. He had spared him things infinitely worse than death.

Susan had arrived so late that my friend had not been woken. Now I had to go to her. I walked into her bedroom wondering how to say it. But it was not difficult; she was a woman of great understanding and generosity, but she found it difficult to express her feelings. This made it easy and we sat side by side, talking quietly.

Then she suddenly turned to me and said, 'Edith, would you like to go and live in my little house in London?'

Though I already knew I could not bear to stay on in Devon, I thanked her as best I could and told her I would like time to think about it. That is how eventually my life turned once again into quiet waters and I came back to London.

During these quiet years I have done much pondering in 'the parlour of my mind'. I came to face squarely that I had been a reluctant missionary. Had I been made of sterner stuff, like my Father and Alfred, I would have been cycling the paths of Africa in my sola topi to this day. But there is a price to be paid for dedicated selfless service such as Father and Alfred gave to Africa and I knew now I had never been willing to pay that price. Self-will had blinded my eyes.

20

TO WALK IN GRACE

MICHAEL WOOD, a young doctor at the Middlesex Hospital, married Susan that year, 1943. With his understanding and compassionate nature it was not surprising that he became a real son to me. They lived with me in London while he worked for his Fellowship of the Royal College of Surgeons.

With the end of the war they decided to live and work abroad. Perhaps it was the influence of the past which drew them to Africa. The two of them and their small family left for East Africa in 1947 and there Michael first practised as a general surgeon and then became a plastic surgeon.

Latterly he has built up an organization which, among a number of enterprises, undertook to run a Flying Doctor Service for East Africa.[1] Knit together by a radio network connected to many outlying mission hospitals, planes can take specialists to assist the hard-pressed medical officer on the spot. Or at times emergencies can be flown to the big hospitals at the various medical centres of East Africa. In one year the small aircraft flew a distance equal to five times the earth's circumference, and the number of operations successfully completed in bush hospitals by him and a growing team of men and women, can now be numbered in hundreds.

1. The African Medical and Research Foundation. Supported by voluntary contributions in Britain, Europe and America.

Michael and Susan have four children, now grown up.

Contrary to the present-day trend to break away from parents and home, these children have a strong devotion to their parents, their home and Africa. All have now finished their education in England, and want to make their home in Africa. All have a sense that they have come into this world to serve, to leave it a better place than when they arrived. I have often asked myself how these parents have succeeded when so many fail, and I consider myself among the latter. Perhaps it is that every holiday they give themselves up to living *with* their children and doing things *with* their children.

Their home is a simple one, made of stone in a cottage pattern. There is the whole farm to roam over and their interests are legion. Added to this, there are twist parties at night or camping parties to some nearby place, where they shoot for the pot, or fish for trout, sleeping at night in the open under a wide starry sky. There may be a trek into Masailand with the medical unit (a big bus affair) which carries everything from a quinine pill to an operating couch, electric dynamo for light, a sterilizer for instruments, and a unit to give films at night to the astonished inhabitants.

It has bred in them a love of open spaces and a love of nature; you feel they have a kinship with one another and the lovely world around them.

I have paid several visits to Michael and Susan in both Kenya and Tanzania during the twenty years they have lived in Africa. My last visit to them was to their farm in Tanzania. It lies 6,000 feet high on the northern slopes of Kilimanjaro. From my window in the wooden cottage I looked out over a well-tended garden of lawns and trees, of roses and arum lilies, and shrubs of every shade of green. Beyond this lay cultivated fields with clumps of shady trees here and there. The wheat sprouted a pale green; on the right a field of pyrethrum the colour of delicate jade. A path ran through these fields, and two ant-like figures crawled along it. The view fell away in a gentle gradient and then suddenly stopped abruptly and dropped, path and all, apparently sheer into the desert hundreds of feet below. Here the scene was one that might have been on the surface of some star. Forty miles of rock and thorn scrub ended in mountains of volcanic structure, which blasted themselves into existence aeons ago. Seen at a distance, the harshness of this landscape has blended into colours as muted as any ancient tapestry. Here and there the desert melted into palest gold, with tints of rose, blue and amethyst and bands of silver glittered where the soda streams lay. Passing clouds threw shadows over the land, blending from charcoal to dove grey. The roughness of the stony ground, the rocks and boulders, and the twisted thorn trees had all been woven into a smooth carpet of loveliness.

Just so I look back now on my life. The rocks and deserts have receded into a timeless landscape to which memory lends a haunting beauty.

When I began to write this last chapter, I found every paragraph began with, 'I know'. But when we say, 'I know', we put ourselves at the bar of the greatest tribunal of all. The judge says, 'You know? What do you know? You know just as much of God's truth as you have love for your fellowmen and *no more*.'

Florence Allshorn in her *Notebooks*[1] says:

> Sift out your own self-gratifications, until you yourself are not very important any more to yourself; but in you there is growing a self that is consciously loved and

1. The *Notebooks* of Florence Allshorn, S.C.M. Press.

loving, gaining an ever-growing peace and sureness and a real joy that no one can take from you.

So I will begin on a gentler tone.

Everything that has happened to me seems to point to there being no death. There is always the beyond—new life, new hope. The corn of wheat falls into the ground and apparently dies, but the day comes when the fresh green of new life appears. We waste our emotions in dread of death, *who* is really a friend of whom few of us are worthy. The end of this life is no stopping-place but a translation of our poor lives into a new dimension of activity in eternity. This spiritual truth seems to have become part of my very being.

I believe it is essential to recognize that God is love in action and not merely a religion; and that I must let Him choose the way in which He will express that love through me. Judging by the way He has created us—and everything else in the world—He must love diversity. Each of our faces is different, even each individual finger-print is different. Surely then in the spiritual realm we should not expect uniformity either.

I like to think that all my life God has been teaching me to be tolerant with those holding different views from my own. I feel we should try to recognize the Kingdom of God in others, even if they may not acknowledge Him themselves. It may show itself in different forms, but is always recognizable by integrity and acts of compassion.

At the time of Alfred's death, I was forty-eight. The children had gone to war service. Out of my failure I had to face learning to live on my own. I found the lesson took a matter of years, not months. I went to a farm in Devonshire and settled down for two months. I faced the first morning with something like panic. I took paper and pencil and wrote myself out a schedule for the day. Every day was the same. I disciplined myself to keep to times and to do the things I actually set out to do. I found the days flew by. This was my first step towards coming out of that loneliness that can lead to despair. And what a surprise awaits one to find that this burden of solitude which took so many years to live with has, *in acceptance,* become the pillow upon which in my old age I can lay my head.

I wish I had learned earlier about forgiveness, both giving and receiving it, and the freedom of spirit it can bring. You cannot have a happy old age without it. My daughter once wrote these words: 'When a situation has broken down in hurt and bitterness, and disagreement is so deep there seems no solution on earth—there remains forgiveness.'

Through our absorption with this business of life, we play in the shallows and have lost the depth dimension. Laying aside traditional language, we need to go deep down into things, the things that really concern us, and face up to those unsolved conflicts within, the uncertainties and disturbances of our inner life. We need to look long and deep into the smallness and the emptiness of life and face our fears. These may be fears of annihilation, fear of death, even fear of life itself. Then there are the guilt feelings that perhaps lie deepest of all. And into these black depths Christ comes to lighten our darkness, to take us by the hand and lead us to the love and mercy of God. In that moment of openness and acceptance of our smallness, our fears and guilt, we are released and receive the grace to live life to its completion.

Sometimes in a crisis I have accepted as if I really knew something of the truths which I have so longed to make my own. At other times—all too many—I have reacted as if I had not learnt anything at all; sending me seeking again my lost treasure.

Then there is the need for a capacity for peace. We need to think, dare to be still and give time for the small miracle of new thought to come to life in our mind, piecing together our scattered thoughts into a continuing purpose. In these days we are so blinded by rush we have no time to savour this beautiful world. No time to listen with the heart; no time to *look* at one another and really *see* one another; no time to break through our reserve and stand with the other fellow in his trouble; no time for little acts of loving doing; no time to speak our love. Great events have hung upon a tear, but we have no time to shed the tears that melt hearts grown hard and brittle in the headlong scramble of life.

Perhaps there is still time—time left to learn. And there is so much to learn—learning to accept each day as it comes, at peace when the day is over; loving God through loving my neighbour; and, finally, to know that fulfilment which comes from learning to walk in grace. And this grace must be taken new every morning from the very hand of God.